Visibly (and Invisibly) Muslim on Grounds

Working and Writing for Change
Series Editors: Steve Parks and Jessica Pauszek

The Working and Writing for Change series began during the 100th anniversary celebrations of NCTE. It was designed to recognize the collective work of teachers of English, Writing, Composition, and Rhetoric to work within and across diverse identities to ensure the field recognize and respect language, educational, political, and social rights of all students, teachers, and community members. While initially solely focused on the work of NCTE/CCCC Special Interest Groups and Caucuses, the series now includes texts written by individuals in partnership with other communities struggling for social recognition and justice.

Books in the Series

CCCC/NCTE Caucuses
Viva Nuestro Caucus: Rewriting the Forgotten Pages of Our Caucus ed. by Romeo García, Iris D. Ruiz, Anita Hernández & María Paz Carvajal Regidor
History of the Black Caucus National Council Teachers of English by Marianna White Davis
Listening to Our Elders: Working and Writing for Social Change by Samantha Blackmon, Cristina Kirklighter, & Steve Parks
Building a Community, Having a Home: A History of the Conference on College Composition and Communication ed. by Jennifer Sano-Franchini, Terese Guinsatao Monberg, & K. Hyoejin Yoon

Community Publications
Visibly (and Invisibly) Muslin on Grounds: Classroom, Culture, and Community at the University of Virginia, ed. by Wafa Salah and Fawzia Tahsin
The Lived Experience of Democracy: Criticizing Injustice, Building Community, ed. by Kaitlyn Baker, et al.
Steal the Street: The Intersection of Homelessness and Gentrification by Mark Mussman
Literacy and Pedagogy in an Age of Misinformation and Disinformation ed. by Tara Lockhart, Brenda Glascott, Chris Warnick, Juli Parrish, & Justin Lewis
Faces of Courage: Ten Years of Building Sanctuary by Harvey Finkle
Equality and Justice: An Engaged Generation, a Troubled World by Michael Chehade, Alex Granner, Ahmed Abdelhakim Hachelaf, Madhu Napa, Samantha Owens, & Steve Parks
Other People's English: Code-Meshing, Code-Switching, and African American Literacy by Vershawn Ashanti Young, Rusty Barrett, Y'Shanda Young-Rivera, & Kim Brian Lovejoy
Becoming International: Musings on Studying Abroad in America, ed.by Sadie Shorr-Parks
Dreams and Nightmares: I Fled Alone to the United States When I Was Fourteen by Liliana Velásquez. ed. and trans. by Mark Lyon
The Weight of My Armor: Creative Nonfiction and Poetry by the Syracuse Veterans' Writing Group, ed. by Ivy Kleinbart, Peter McShane, & Eileen Schell
PHD to PhD: How Education Saved My Life by Elaine Richardson

Visibly (and Invisibly) Muslim on Grounds

CLASSROOM, CULTURE, AND COMMUNITY AT
THE UNIVERSITY OF VIRGINIA

Edited by
Wafa Salah
Fawzia Tahsin

Parlor Press
Anderson, South Carolina
www.parlorpress.com

Parlor Press LLC, Anderson, South Carolina, USA
Copyright © 2023 by New City Community Press

Printed in the United States of America on acid-free paper.

Library of Congress Cataloging-in-Publication Data on File

1 2 3 4 5

978-1-64317-398-6 (paperback)
978-1-64317-399-3 (PDF)

Working and Writing for Change
An Imprint Series of Parlor Press
Series Editors: Steve Parks and Jessica Pauszek

Cover image by Dalia Gokce
Interior design by Justin Lewis, justalewis1@gmail.com

Parlor Press, LLC is an independent publisher of scholarly and trade titles in print and multimedia formats. This book is available in paper and eBook formats from Parlor Press on the World Wide Web at www.parlorpress.com or through online and brick-and-mortar bookstores. For submission information or to find out about Parlor Press publications, write to Parlor Press, 3015 Brackenberry Drive, Anderson, South Carolina, 29621, or email editor@parlorpress.com.

Beginnings

Fadumo Hussein

As a Muslim, as a woman, and as a Black person, I think my experiences are fundamental to understanding UVA. I want to bring awareness to those experiences and hopefully solve some issues at UVA. There aren't many spaces where I feel represented, so why not a book?

J. H.

I remember walking out and feeling so good that a teacher would ask me, in a class with 50 other students, what it's like to wear a hijab on campus, you know? But, like, white students that live in a carefree world, most of them, they've never faced racial tension, racial hatred from people, mistreatment. Sometimes the "best" thing these students can do is to stop *you* from talking so that *they* could be saved from being reminded that *we* have been treated as if we have lower status, that we have been treated that way. They want you to move on, but how are you going to move on if you don't talk about what's affecting you? I want to talk about what it's like to be a hijabi on UVA Grounds.

Y. H.

It's always good to talk about important issues. Putting your ideas out there, putting your pain out there, based on your experiences and beliefs, is a positive. When it comes to what we can do and who we can collaborate with on issues facing our community, representing ourselves is always a positive.

K. S.

I think it's important for Muslim Americans to talk about their experiences and to just have their voices heard. It's like you have a group of people who identify as the same thing, but they don't necessarily agree with each other on everything. If your voice is heard, though, you could have conversations with each other. It's important for Muslims to have a platform even if they disagree with each other, even if their opinions are completely different. At UVA, I think, you are allowed to change your opinion as a Muslim, you're allowed to grow and learn and be more confident in your faith.

Narjes Bencheikh

It's important for us to put ourselves out there. To not be afraid to join University Guides, to join Honor, to apply to live on The Lawn, to apply to be RAs. Muslim representation is increasing every year. There's maybe, like 20 Muslim RAs. There's two Muslims living on The Lawn. I know we have people in Honor. Yes, the Muslim Student Association is a good time, but we should put ourselves out there in all the organizations. We should be out there with our peers. With this book, we can tell ourselves and future Muslims that there's nothing that should hold us back.

Ahmed Hussain

I liked the idea of just reaching out to more Muslims. I don't know if this book is specifically going to do that, maybe it will. I don't really know, but I like the idea of it. I think that idea harkens back to when I was a kid. No one was around to help me, to relate to me, or to be a role model for me. Today, it's different. There are people like Hasan Minhaj, who is a Muslim in mainstream media. He's a really good role model for a lot of people. Before him, there wasn't really anyone prominent I could look up to in Western media, whereas white kids could look up to every celebrity, whether it was in entertainment, business, or science. I feel in our culture there's this idea of being middle of the road, settling for good enough. As long as you're doing something respectable and staying out of trouble, you're fine. You shouldn't want to be in the spotlight. You shouldn't need to be doing anything extra. Why do you need all of these people's eyes on you? But maybe that attention can contribute to someone's idea of Muslim students. This book project opened my eyes to the idea that maybe people with experiences like mine can benefit from Muslims being in the spotlight a little bit more.

Rawan Osman

When you asked me to be part of this book about Muslim students at UVA, I thought, "Yes, this is definitely something I want to talk about." It's something very important. The more that people can know how Muslim students feel, as well as how other marginalized students feel, the better they will be able to respond to our needs and the inequities in our experiences. Right now, things are not good. People are not comfortable here and do not feel welcomed. Things need to change. I'm not saying every Muslim student has a responsibility to speak up for themselves. No Muslim student should have to do that work. It's very much a burden. It's exhausting. However, I'm willing and want to put myself out there to make things better for Muslim students. This project seems to be a wonderful platform. I just really hope that this publication gets to the right people in the administration and that they truly take this seriously to make Muslim students and other marginalized students feel more comfortable here. Not surface-level changes just to say "we did something," but deep, radical, and positive institutional changes.

Omer Gorashi

I'm here to help, however I can. Although I myself may not have something in particular that I want to share, the least I can do is be a part of something that's larger, even if it just merely adds to what another person has shared. And all of our shared experiences together can then maybe get the school's attention through this work. The fact that you're doing this, I'm already like, "Okay! There are people that are working towards getting Muslims heard, getting Black Muslims heard and represented!"

Ilyas Saltani

We're starting to advocate for ourselves and have an opinion on issues that are influencing our students. A lot of times, when decisions are made, people in the room do not really consider that there are different identities that will respond to different initiatives. Muslim students, who have experienced a level of marginalization, in that sense, can advocate for marginalized communities. No matter how much you study it in a vacuum, as a white student, you won't get the socio-emotional aspect of that experience. It's not something that you can learn or read about. It's something that you feel. A lot of times it's even indescribable. It's understanding social cues or mannerisms in ways that you interact and engage with other people that makes you feel marginalized. There are things that you just won't understand unless you've experienced them. Being able to vocalize that in a larger space and having the platform to advocate for your people in that way, is huge. I'm still proud of our community for being able to do that. It's inspiring!

Sumaya Mohammed

When I saw your research topic I thought that this is something that we really need. This is something that Muslims coming into UVA need to see before getting here, just so they can look forward to the experience, have the dos and don'ts of attending UVA as a Muslim, and just have their peers and predecessors give them advice on what to expect. If I had read this book before coming to UVA, I definitely would have had a more positive mindset coming in. I would know where to find my people, where to look or where to go, the spaces to get involved in, because finding your space at UVA can be very much a trial and error otherwise.able to do that. It's inspiring!

CONTENTS

XII   COMMON UVA TERMINOLOGY

XIV   ACKNOWLEDGMENTS

XVIII   INTRODUCTION
Wafa Salah and Fawzia Tahsin

XXXIX TIMELINE OF RELEVANT EVENTS AS CITED BY UVA STUDENT
PARTICIPANTS

PART I: CLASSROOMS

3   Ayah Mahdi, "Muslims Are Not a Monolith"

*Further Reflections: Faris Musa, Palwasha Ayyub, F.C., Narjes
Bencheikh, K.S., R.M., Javaria Abbasi*

17   Noor Samee, "I Have Always Been Both the Student and the
Teacher"

*Further Reflections: Sara Ali, J.H., M.B., Javaria Abbasi, Narjes Bencheikh,
P.E., Isata Kamara*

29   R.M., "I Was Hurt. I Felt Like My Voice Wasn't Being Heard
about How Offensive That Act Was to Me"

Further Reflections: Fadumo Hussein, Javaria Abbasi, K.S.

37   T.J., "It's Getting More Difficult to Publicly Identify As a Muslim"

Further Reflections: M.B., Javaria Abbasi, K.S., Sara Ali, P.E., Faris Musa, K.G.

49   K.G., "I Think Certain Sections Are Definitely Improving"

Further Reflections: Y.H., M. Ahmad

PART II: CULTURE

55   C.P., "The Climate Here Is Exhausting to Students of Color"

Further Reflections: M.B., Mazzen Shalaby

64   Rawan Osman, "Carrying the Burden of Promoting Diversity and Inclusion Literally Means That We Can't Invest Our Time Elsewhere"

Further Reflections: K.G., Sara Ali, I.F

75   Ilyas Saltani, "I Can't Believe That Came Out of Your Mouth"

Further Reflections: Shahira Ali, Ahmed Hussain, Fadumo Hussein

87   Khadeja Muhammed, "As a Muslim Myself, It Should Not Be My Responsibility To Figure Out How to Do It for Them"

Further Reflections: Mazzen Shalaby, P.E., Javaria Abbasi, K.G., Y.H.

99   Al Ahmed, "Why Do Students Have to Go Out of Their Way to Push Administrators to Get Things Done?"

Further Reflections: Hisham Ahmad, K.S.

PART III: COMMUNITY

109   Saajid Hasan, "I Think Muslims Have Amazing Potential and Capacity"

115 Hira Azher, "We Tried to Re-imagine a Space for Muslim Students That Prioritizes the Experience of Marginalized Muslims"

125 A.N., "Black Muslims Shouldn't Have to Split Themselves in Two: We're Black and Muslim, not Either/Or"

Further Reflections: Omer Gorashi, Fadumo Hussein

135 Saqib Rizvi, "A Huge Part of Being Muslim is Also Advocating for the Rights of Those That Are Underrepresented and Oppressed"

140 M.M., "Being Comfortable in a Space Means Welcoming Sincerity Over Conformity"

150 Sumaya Mohammed, "My Advice to First Years At a Recent MSA Event: UVA's MSA Is What You Make It"

156 AFTERWORD
Oludamini Ogunnaike, Associate Professor of African Religious Thought and Democracy, Dept. of Religious Studies, University of Virginia

169 NOTES

161 GLOSSARY OF KEY TERMS

170 EDITOR BIOGRAPHIES

Common UVA Terminology

A-School – School of Architecture
Batten – Frank Batten School of Leadership and Public Policy
BSA – Black Student Alliance
CIO – Contracted Independent Organization
Comm School – The McIntire School of Commerce
E-School – School of Engineering and Applied Sciences
EESA - Ethiopia and Eritrea Student Association
DACA – Deferred Action for Childhood Arrivals
DREAMers – Supports of the DREAM (Development, Relief, and Education
        for Alien Minors) Act
GDS – Global Development Studies
Grounds – The term used by generations of students, faculty, and alumni to
        refer to the University premises, rather than "Campus"
Honor – The UVA Honor Code System exists to uphold and support the
        Community Trust. Students pledge to never lie, steal or cheat.[1]
HRL – Housing and Residence Life
ISCV - Islamic Society of Central Virginia
JPA – Jefferson Park Avenue
L2K – Leadership 2K
LSC – Lawn Selection Committee
MESA – Middle Eastern South Asian
MILE – The Muslim Institute for Leadership and Empowerment
MSA – Muslim Student Association
MU – Muslims United
OAAA – Office of African American Affairs
PULSE – Perspective, Understanding, Leadership, Sustained Exchange
        chapter at UVA

---

1   https://honor.virginia.edu/overview

PWI – Predominantly White Institution
QSU – Queer Student Union
RAs – Resident Advisors
SEAS - School of Engineering & Applied Sciences
SOR – Sigma Omicron Rho; a social fraternity for the LGBTQ+ community
Student Self Governance - The notion that common university decision
     making is entrusted to students[2]
The Lawn - A popular community gathering spot in front of the Rotunda;
     can also refer to students who live in Lawn rooms
UJC – University Judiciary Committee
undocUVA – CIO focused on advocating for undocumented students
VCU – Virginia Commonwealth University
WGS – Women and Gender Studies

---

[2] https://www.virginia.edu/life/selfgovernance

Acknowledgments

We want to begin by thanking all the Muslim students who trusted us to hear and then to share their personal stories with readers of this book. Without their courage to speak the project would not have been possible. We are also indebted to the UVA Muslim Student Association, who early in this project supported our efforts to reach out to the Muslim student community. This project's completion also would not have been possible without the monetary support of the UVA Harrison Grant, UVA College Council Grant, and the Jefferson Trust. We also want to thank UVA's Undergraduate Office of Research (OUR) for their Undergraduate Student Opportunities for Academic Research (USOAR) program, out of which this project emerged. We want to thank Andrus G. Ashoo, Director of OUR and Melissa Hey, Former Assistant Director of OUR for their academic and personal support of this USOAR project. We would like to thank Professor Oludamini Ogunnaike, Associate Professor of African Religious Thought and Democracy in the UVA Department of Religious Studies for his feedback and contribution to writing the afterword. We also would like to thank Jannatul Pramanik, Former Assistant Director for Multicultural Student Services for her persistent support and work for the Muslim community and other multicultural communities on UVA grounds. As this project neared completion, we also received important insights from student and faculty reviewers within UVA and across the United States. We have also benefited from the work of the English Department's Stacey Trader, Sarah Arrington, and Kate Stephenson. Without their dedication, we would not have been able to navigate UVA bureaucracy to use the dedicated grants to complete this project. Maizie Jackson provided essential guidance as we navigated the Internal Review Board approval process. We would also like to express our sincere gratitude to Imam

Abd'Llah Al-Ansari, who helped provide the definitions of the key Islamic terms cited, ensuring accurate representation.

Finally, our deepest thanks goes to our mentor, advisor, and greatest ally, Professor Stephen J. Parks. His unwavering support and dedication helped make this project a reality. Without his academic guidance, mentorship, and personal support, this publication would not have been possible. He helped us find our voice and assert it confidently. It is crucial to recognize how important it was to him that we had full control of our project and that he was to step in only if we needed or asked for it. We were afforded the full autonomy of telling our community's story and, in doing so, we learned to advocate for ourselves, our peers, and our community as a whole. Moreover, Prof. Parks ensured that we were always fully compensated for our time and efforts. We truly could not have asked for a better, kinder, more humble and genuine advisor. It is his persistent belief in our efforts and abilities that helped bring this project to where it is today. For all this and more, we are eternally grateful to him and his guidance.

To acknowledge the labor and insights the students provided to this project, a portion of the proceeds from sales of Visibly (and Invisibly) Muslim will be used to support undergraduate Muslim student organizations at the University of Virginia.

Wafa Salah

Alhamdulillah! All praise belongs to Allah.

I want to thank my parents, Seid and Zafaran, without whom I would not be where I am today. To my mother, Zafaran, I want to dedicate this book and my work. Anything and everything that I accomplish is to her credit. I owe all of my successes to her unwavering love, support, and sacrifice that she continues to make to this day. It is from her that I learned the meaning of hard work, resilience, and the unwillingness to give up when faced with challenges. Her strength and grace fuel my being and motivate me to pursue my dreams. Thank you, mom, for being the best mother, friend, and role-model that a girl could ever ask for.

I would also like to thank my brother, Hesham, who has been the most reliable presence in my life. He has always been and continues to be the person that I could count on for anything and everything. Much of what I have done would not have been possible without his unconditional support and counsel. It is a blessing to have him as a brother, and I am forever grateful to him and all the dreams that he helped make come true.

Furthermore, I would like to thank my sisters Nawal, Ida, and Hannan for their constant cheer and encouragement with all my endeavors. I will never forget everything that you have done for me and all the struggles that you have gone through which undoubtedly made my path forward easier. I also want to thank my brothers-in-law, who have always been there for me whenever I needed their help. To my nephew, Mikey, thank you for being you and for always willing to share your true thoughts with me. Finally, to my little nieces and nephews, my favorite little humans in the world, thank you for inspiring me to always push for and help create a kinder and more accepting world for you and your generation.

I am thankful to my oldest, closest, and sincerest friends, Raniya and Hanin. They have always been there to pick me up at my lowest and cheer me on through my highest points in life. I am thankful for the years of love, kindness, and support that you both have shown me, all of which has helped shape me into the person that I am today. I am lucky to have you both in my life, and I am indebted to our friendship and bond.

To two of my incredible and closest friends, Beza and Makdes, I also want to give my heartfelt thanks. Our experiences at UVA and deep conversations have significantly shaped how I think, perceive, understand, and react to the environment around me. They not only helped me in always seeing various perspectives but also in better understanding mine. The memories we shared as well as your unwavering love and encouragement are things that I will always cherish.

My deepest gratitude goes to one of my closest and kindest friends, Aisha Singh. I want to thank her for her endless support, encouragement, and reassurance. Throughout the life of this project, she has been there to actively listen, offer insights, and give me feedback whenever I needed it. Thank you for always asking, listening, and just matching my excitement about the promise and potential of this project. I am eternally grateful to you and your friendship.

Finally, to all my family, friends, and mentors that have supported me in one form or another through the years and have always believed in my abilities even at times that I doubted myself, I am forever grateful to you and all the kindness that you have shown me.

Fawzia Tahsin

"So, surely with hardship comes ease" (Quran 94:5)

I want to first start off by thanking my parents. My mom and dad, Shahana and Mohammad, helped shape me into the person I am today. They sacrificed to immigrate to a new country without speaking its language. They showed persistent effort to work multiple jobs tirelessly to support their children's education and dreams. They have always been there to support, encourage, and challenge me. Special thanks to my mother for her unwavering love for anything I set my mind to. If there is anyone whose actions speak louder than words it is my mother. Her kindness and warmth are always felt in everything she does. She sacrificed her dreams to better the lives of her children. My mother lives and does everything for her children. Being her only daughter is something I wear with pride.

I want to thank my older brothers as well, Mohammad N. and Mohammad R. My brothers bore numerous hardships to help me build the future I want. They have supported my academic ambitions, physically, financially, and emotionally. They have worked tirelessly to support our family financially and physically. Being the younger and only sister, I will always appreciate the life perspectives they have passed down to me. All in all, I will always be grateful for my family's support both seen and unseen. They are the bedrock that instilled in me the values of resilience, kindness, and gratefulness. They are why I can advocate for the communities I care about. They are also the reason why I practice my faith with pride and confidence.

Last but not least, I want to acknowledge my friends' love and support. Both near and far, thank you all for always cheering me on and pushing me forward. You all know who you are and I appreciate you all more than you will ever know. From listening to my various rants, encouraging me when I was feeling down, being the shoulder I can cry on, and advocating for my academic and career goals. I can never repay the kindness you all have shown me.

Furthermore, I would like to thank UVA professors and staff for their contributions and support for this book. To all supporters and readers of this book, thank you as well. This project is and will continue to be the highlight of my college career and beyond.

SubhanAllah (Glory be to God)!

Introduction

Wafa Salah and Fawzia Tahsin

Intertwined Beginnings

Fawzia Tahsin: It was in 6th grade when I first started to wear the hijab. To be quite honest, I didn't understand the true meaning of hijab and why I wore it. I just wore it because my religion said I must. I soon realized, though, how much of my identity had changed. I remember all my friends gave me strange but curious looks the first day of school. Many of my friends did not talk to me. Others were unusually quiet towards me. I noticed I was also becoming a lot quieter. Every day I was trembling with fear over the thought that people were silently judging me. At that point, I wasn't 100 percent comfortable with the hijab. It was something I loved and hated at the same time. I loved it because I knew I was doing the right thing by following my faith, but I hated it because I wasn't blending in with the rest of my classmates. I was the odd one out. Eventually, I adapted to it, but I still felt like I was walking on thin ice. Many people don't seem to realize it, but it takes courage to put the hijab on every day.

Growing up, I attended a Hispanic-majority elementary and middle school. After middle school, I attended a predominantly-white high school. The school was brand new. I was in 10th grade when it opened. All the clubs and organizations had to be made from scratch. A few Muslim girls decided to start a Muslim Student Association (MSA), and I was elected to be the secretary that year. It was hard to find a sponsor and a room in which to meet after school. What made it harder, though, was we received absolutely no funding from our high school. The next year, I was the MSA president. I would go to the school administration office to receive permission to raise funds for group activities. Every time, my request was rejected. Their explanation was that religious-affiliated organizations could not raise funds on school property. It was against the school's rules. This made no sense to me as many other high school MSAs across the school county raised funds. Our club also received very little support from staff. We were left to do things on our own. At that time, I didn't think much of it. I just thought "It is, what it is." But not feeling supported was hard on our members, who not only had no social events like the rest of their peers, but no place to experience community. In hindsight, I realized how much we were made to struggle to create a safe space where Muslims could join together to discuss important issues within our community.

Wafa Salah: Feeling welcomed, gaining a sense of belonging, being a part of something – I mean truly a part and not a mere contributor from the outside-- are natural and innate desires that we all, as humans, possess. In whatever it is that we do, humans have this innate longing to belong. That is especially true for college students who leave their home community often to live in a completely new environment. Like all students, the question of "Who am I" is a question that Muslim students must grapple with when leaving for college. Growing up, familial influence plays a huge role in our decision making, even small ones like who we hang out with or how we spend our Friday nights. So, to be on our own for the first time, without familial voices influencing our every move, is a new undertaking. It is the beginning of when we discover ourselves outside of the context of the family and the culture in which we were raised.

This route to self-discovery, however, becomes intertwined and increasingly confusing when outside societal pressures keep trying to box us into their stereotypes of Muslims. Most college students will find themselves asking, "Will I be able to make friends? How will my classes go? How much of myself should I really reveal? Should I just take on an entire new persona in an attempt to 'fit in'? Who even am I?" The internal and social struggles that we had as teenagers in high school follow us, to some extent, into this new chapter in our lives. For Muslim students in America, however, there is an additional worry; a mind-numbing stressor that we are forced to grapple with on the weeks leading up to move-in day. This anxiety is even more pronounced when one is coming to a predominantly white institution (PWI) like the University of Virginia (UVA).

The question of "Will they accept me for who I am?" is a daunting one for Muslim students. In a post 9/11 world, where the words "Muslim" and "terrorist" are all but synonymous, Muslims have been unjustly and inaccurately cast as threats to the fundamental American values of freedom and liberty. Such stereotypes necessarily become part of a university student culture. It is the culture most U.S. students are raised within from childhood, through their early schooling, and into college. Add to this culture the fact that Muslims are not supposed to drink or "party" in the traditional sense, then all that remains is a large neon sign painting Muslim students as "American College Social Outcasts." This is even more the case for a hijab-wearing woman whose identity becomes reduced to the westerner's idea of oppression. Us hijabis, we really stand no chance at fitting or blending in. All these thoughts are additional worries that plague the Muslim first-year's mind on move-in day.

Sadly, it does not end there. The psychological fear pales in comparison to the very real physical threats that we face. I remember when Nabra Hassanen was sexually assaulted then killed in 2017 near the All Dulles Area Muslim Society (ADAMS) Center, during Ramadan, Islam's holiest month of the year[3]. This was too close to home for a lot of Muslim women. It was especially close to home for visibly Muslim women at UVA, who predominantly come from Northern Virginia (NoVA) and had likely been involved in the ADAMS Center for a good portion of their lives. Every NoVA's Muslim woman and her parents were on edge after hearing that horrendous news. For us, the issue was not so much whether the assault could officially be classified as a "hate crime." The attack on Hassanen stands for a constant psychological fear of standing out from other students. I remember getting a call from relatives from all over telling me to be careful with my hijab. Perhaps, it was suggested, "I should even consider switching to wearing a hoodie or a beanie so that I can 'blend in' as an American." We are constantly reminded that being safe means making who we are less visible.

---

3 On June 18, 2017, Nabra Hassanen, a 17-year-old Muslim American girl from Reston, Virginia, was sexually assaulted and murdered by Darwin Martinez Torres. He was indicted for Hassanen's rape and murder and subsequently pleaded guilty to both charges. In March 2019, he was sentenced to eight consecutive life terms in prison for the crimes. Police identified the killing as an act of road rage, and not a hate crime. (Al Jazeera. June 20, 2017.)

This constant need to be aware of how others "see" us impacts how we understand what are usually everyday events. I remember an evening where a friend and I went to a restaurant to grab dinner. It was about forty-five minutes before the restaurant closed --we didn't know this at the time. It was the weekend, so the place was packed. The hosts told us that it would be about a 20-minute wait, but they could put us on the waitlist and then text us when our table was ready. We could also wait at the bar. We were already hungry, but my friend really liked that restaurant and wanted me to try it. We decided to put our names down and just walk around in the neighborhood until our table was ready. As we headed out, I noticed this large group of people coming in to be seated. I thought to myself, "Poor them, their wait is going to be even longer. There's barely any room in this place for two let alone that many." As my friend and I made our way out, I heard them ask the hostess how long the wait would be for a table.

We walked around for quite a bit, caught each other up on all the new things in our lives. Time had flown and we were starving at this point. It had been over forty minutes. My friend hadn't received a text about our table. We decided to go back and check. The same two girls were at the host stand, so we asked about our table and said we had not received a text from the restaurant. They told us that the kitchen had closed, but that they could seat us at the bar. Then I saw that the large group of people were not only seated, but already eating appetizers. I was livid! There were so many thoughts racing through my mind: If we had not come to check for ourselves, were they really just going to make us wait for a table that would never be ready? Did she really just ask us for a second time --two hijabis-- if we wanted to go and sit at the bar? Knowing that the kitchen was closed so getting drinks was the only option? And the main trigger of them all: why on earth is that large group of people who came after us, whom I know had no reservations, sitting and eating while we, technically, should have been sat first?

But I didn't yell. I didn't demand to speak to a manager. I was just disgusted at that point. I didn't want to waste energy on a place that didn't value me as a guest. It was not just their actions that made me feel unwelcome. It was their tone, their manner of speaking, their blatant unconcern for their mistake. It was their rush to shove us into the bar area, to find a solution "for us," for the "hijabis."

Now, was it actually related to our hijab? There is no way to know for sure. In fact, I had considered the possibility that I might have just misinterpreted the situation. Truth be told, I did not feel any active malice coming from their side, just unconcern. Unconcern that left me feeling like a second-class citizen, a non-priority; a disheartening realization that as a minority, my rights will only matter if and only if there is no one "more important" around. I wondered repeatedly after that night, would this have happened to a non-minority? And if it had, would those hostesses have displayed the same kind of heedlessness and blatant unconcern as they did to us? The culmination of all my past experiences says, "Probably not!" But there is no way for me to show that their actions were, in fact, tied to our minority identity, our Muslim identity.

I guess I could ask them openly if they harbor any anti-Muslim sentiments. But I am almost certain it would only result in their feeling shocked at such a question or accusation, followed immediately by an "Of course not!" After all, there is nothing overtly Islamophobic about what they said or did. However, to me, this type of Islamophobia – the obscure kind – is the hardest one to combat, because the person is not even aware of its existence. You learn to avoid the open Islamophobes. There are other people, however, who will tell you (and tell themselves) that they harbor no negative feelings towards you or your identity. Eventually though, some event unfolds, and you realize that their actions, conscious or otherwise, don't align with what they claim. What's worse, you cannot even openly discuss that with them, because "They obviously did not mean it that way" and "YOU are just overreacting."

So, my response was not just based on the actual event, but a recurring feeling. That feeling when a hijabi student's ideas get dismissed in an evolutionary-biology class discussion merely because it is assumed that the hijabi doesn't believe in evolution. It's the feeling when an entire class assumes your stance, instead of actually asking for your opinion, your thoughts. It is the feeling when "the hall" decides not to invite the one Muslim kid to a social event because it is automatically assumed that he/she/they will be a "prude". The feeling that makes it really hard to figure out who you are. And at those moments, you recognize that the decision-making power you thought you'd get as a college student has actually been handed to the rest of society instead. So, when you are singled out, treated in a manner that you know is not right, what are you supposed to think? How are you supposed to feel? Maybe you are just supposed to make your identity invisible.

Fawzia Tahsin: Coming into UVA, I've realized how much of this sense of being "seen," being cast into harsh stereotypes of Muslim culture, is present at UVA. The harsh reality is that I cannot easily exist in a predominantly white space. I always have to be on edge. During class, when there are discussions about terrorism, people will always look at me to defend my religion and re-state (again) that terrorism is not the meaning of Islam. Even during actual religious discussions, I feel as if I'm not learning anything valuable. It's all textbook lecturing with no discussion of Islam's actual beliefs or its values. As a result, people will continue to make insensitive comments not realizing how their words can affect Muslim students' sense of identity, belonging, and safety. And I will continue to have to smile and present myself as overly-approachable just to counteract or neutralize the threat that is incorrectly associated with my Muslim identity. I will have to continue to defend Islam every time somebody foolish decides to do something heinous and attribute that act to my religion. And I will continue to be unable to speak about certain political topics or criticize the US government's foreign policy simply to not come off as un-American.

Wafa Salah: Of course, I've also had great allies at UVA. I've had non-Muslim friends who invited me to their party and have everyone play a drinking game with water, just so I wouldn't feel left out. They knew I couldn't play if it involved drinking alcohol. I've had non-Muslim friends who, while studying in the library, would remind me to go and pray if ever I was lost in work and forgot. Runk Dining Hall staff, who, upon my walking in, would tell me right away which food stations to avoid because they contained pork. That same staff would allow me to go and pray in the manager's office --where no student is allowed-- if I happened to be there at prayer time. There were people like Mama Kathy who would always greet me with a big hug and an "Assalamu Alaikum" which always made me feel loved and at home.

Fawzia Tahsin: I still remember the first time I attended a Muslim Student Association (MSA) general body meeting at UVA. Ever since my arrival, I had been trying to find my niche in this school. I attended a few club meetings here and there based on my interest, but it all seemed very cliquey. I thought it would be difficult to connect with the UVA Muslim community since it is not the largest Muslim community when compared to other Virginia colleges. At this meeting, as I entered the big meeting hall, I was one of the first people there, besides my roommate and the executive members. I sat on the edge of the room as I didn't want to draw too much attention to myself. As soon as my roommate sat down, one of the other MSA members immediately came towards us and introduced himself. He was very nice. I could tell he was deeply involved with the MSA community. As more people joined the meeting, I began to feel a bit awkward. Besides my roommate, I had a hard time trying to talk to other people. It seemed like people had already established their social groups. Everything seemed very cliquey again. However, I tried to embrace the awkwardness by striking conversations with some of the other members. I came in with a non-judgmental attitude and tried to be open to new friendships. I wanted to be open to new adventures with, hopefully, my home community for the next four years.

Then executive members began to break us up into small groups and facilitate more conversations through icebreakers and group activities. During these ice breakers, as a Muslim, I tried to understand how we (as Muslims) make sense of our community. How do we navigate the predominantly white spaces at this institution? What are some ways to help uplift our peers into positions of distinguished leadership like Student Council, UVA Honor, University Guide Service, or even higher honors, like living in a Lawn room? How do we assert ourselves into the UVA bureaucratic system so we can facilitate real, equitable change at this university for ourselves and future generations to come? I thought of how an outsider would view this Muslim general body meeting. At first glance, the meeting might seem a testament to self-segregation, a belief that permeates throughout this university that Muslim students, like other minority communities, tend to only stay within their racial groups (e.g., Pakistanis, Arab, Black Muslims, etc.). But, I thought, an outsider may also appreciate the vast diversity of the community coming together through faith. Throughout this general body meeting, I actively listened to the different social conversations to not only better understand my community and our concerns, but to also learn how to address these concerns.

Wafa Salah/Fawzia Tahsin: Our shared experiences, our attempt to listen deeply to our community's experiences and insights, led to the creation of this book. Our goal is to represent the actual Muslim student experience within the culture of UVA, in all its diversity and contradictions. We hope to understand how that complex experience at times represents, and at others contradicts, the rhetoric of diversity and tolerance that envelopes the Grounds. We want to explore what this focus on tolerance looks and feels like within our community. And once a more complete representation of our community is made visible, we want to explore how the university might better respond to its concerns. How might UVA build off the tremendous resources our community brings to "the Grounds"? What might happen if stereotypes of terrorists are replaced with the actualities of our insights and aspirations?

As members of the UVA community and as members of UVA's Muslim community, we felt an obligation to take on this work. Building from the heritage of other communities of color and the labor of other identity-based organizations, we listen to and uplift our community's voices. While focused on the Muslim community in particular, this project is in support of all UVA POC communities in its call for equitable action. All students, faculty, staff, and administrators have a moral obligation to learn and do better. We recognize that growth and progress are impossible without having committed students that support marginalized voices and our collective future. Through listening to and then representing these voices, we believe real change can begin. This is the change we want to envision and support with the pages that follow.

Engaged Conversations

Throughout the over two-year journey of developing this book, we thought about how we could best support Muslim students. We immediately decided our project had to begin with listening to our community. Muslim voices and insights had to be at the core of this project. And to confront simplistic stereotypes, we committed to representing the diversity of opinions and experiences of the Muslim community at UVA. Our intention was not to present an ideological stance, a political agenda, or an emotional rant. Rather our hope was that demonstrating the complexity and diversity of opinion within the Muslim student community would itself be the best argument against stereotypes. It would also be the strongest argument for our community's value to UVA.

As such, you will not find a simple definition of "being Muslim" within these pages. There is not a one-fits-all description. Nor is there a single description of UVA. Rather, there are locations across the Grounds that make a Muslim student feel unwelcome, almost like an intruder. In this book, you will see how Muslim students learn to avoid those places and the people which make them feel that way. But you will also see that Muslim students have their own communities, in whatever way they define them, whether it's a small friend group or a large organization. These are the communities that make the entire UVA experience worth it.

In this book, our role is to neither romanticize nor condemn either end of this spectrum. Life is made in the "messy middle." As such, we enumerate the good, the bad, the neutral, the fascinating, the not-so-interesting, and every other aspect of a Muslim student's experience at UVA. We do so in the hopes that, by representing the full range of what our UVA Muslim community confronts and experiences on a daily basis, the larger UVA community can gain an awareness of how their words and their actions can either open up the space for community or reduce complexity to stereotypes. We hope, then, to make the general student population aware of what the now-dominant ways of speaking and acting on-Grounds indicate to their Muslim peers. And by uncovering the layers of identities that a Muslim inhabits as an individual and that the Muslim community houses as a whole, we attempt to show the diversity, subtleties, and nuances that are often missed when Muslims are stereotyped or grouped into this one thing. Our hope is to create new conversations in which all participate and benefit.

To achieve these goals, our efforts are informed by participant observer, ethnographic research, and oral history strategies. We believed this alignment best represented our belief that the complexity of Muslim student culture would emerge through the stories they tell each other to make sense of their experiences; the stories we have told ourselves. In this way, we also felt that using strategies associated with ethnography allowed us to acknowledge ourselves as participants in this community, but provided tools which allowed a distance, a sense of objectivity, when considering the complex meanings of the stories being collected. As such, we believed ethnographic research methodologies, premised on meaningful conversations with Muslim students, would enable a rich tapestry of experiences to be made visible. We do not claim to have produced an ethnography, however. We just want to make clear we were influenced by such values.

The initial goal of each conversation, then, was to see how unique and different the UVA experience was from one Muslim student to another. Our first step was to develop a rich pool of potential participants. At first, we relied on personal networks in which our motivations would be trusted by those involved. We asked if these students, our friends, would be interested in participating in our project. This initial trusting community served as a basis from which to expand the scope of our project. With Institutional Review Board (IRB) approval, we developed a set of specific research questions, an invitation letter, and a formal process to record as well as store the conversations to ensure privacy for those involved. We then sent the approved letter to various constituencies within our community – individual students, recognized student leaders, and alumni. We also approached UVA's Muslim Student Association to see if they would distribute our letter through their official newsletters or respective social media. Soon enough, the project was officially advertised to over 500 UVA Muslim students. As students reached out to us, we decided there was no reason to deny anyone an opportunity to be heard, so we tried to meet with any student that volunteered to participate. However, in some cases, due to logistical reasons, meetings were never fulfilled.

As noted above, we recognized that the Muslim experience at UVA is very diverse, a diversity marked by each person's unique trajectory through the institution. For that reason, we wanted to ensure we were capturing as many viewpoints as possible. In addition to interviewing volunteers from our general outreach campaign, we also intentionally reached out to a wide array of majors, class years and schools (e.g., Batten, McIntire, Medical, SEAS). We intentionally reached out to Muslim students who represented different cultural, racial, and ethnic heritages as well as different levels of iman. Despite this effort, however, we recognize that South Asian student identity makes up a substantial portion of the book. This is primarily due to the specific demographics at UVA, where African and Black Muslims are not as large a part of the Muslim community, at least in terms of the Muslim community on which our work is partially based. Here we want to recognize how our community is expanding the range of organizations that might represent our diversity, as highlighted in this book. (Of course, not every student belongs to an official organization.) And we hope that UVA will address the seeming lack of support for these specific Muslim communities as it continues to diversify our student body. Yet, we also hope, it is clear that our goal was not to track down specific demographics just for the sake of their identity. Our goal was not to replace one dominant stereotype with a thousand smaller stereotypes. Rather, by actively including different Muslim identities, in all their heritages, we believed the reader will gain a unique glimpse into the life of a UVA Muslim student, not the UVA Muslim student.

For example, our conversations with students often began by asking, "What is the first thing you believe people notice about you?" The goal of this question was to understand how UVA culture (and beyond) initially perceives a Muslim student. Except for the women who wore hijab, whose responses were unsurprisingly "My hijab," the responses were quite varied. For everyone else, that is, the answer was their ethnic background, their race, their gender identity, their manner of speaking, or any other part of their identity that was outwardly obvious. It wasn't exactly "their Islam" that was immediately perceived. Unless one announces his/her/their religious identity, being a Muslim doesn't exactly have a physical marker. All of this is to say that a Muslim woman is also a woman, a Black Muslim is also Black, an immigrant Muslim is also an immigrant, an Arab Muslim is also Arab, and a Desi Muslim is also Desi. And in all cases, a Muslim is a combination of some or all of these identities. It was the specificity of that intersectional experience we sought to represent by seeking out a diverse pool of participants and, by the end of our outreach to the community, we had engaged in many conversations, of which approximately 36 are represented in this collection.

When a student agreed to take part in our project, we scheduled the conversation at a mutually-agreed upon time. Prior to the conversation, all students were briefed on the project, its implications, and the timeline. We also stressed that each person would have editorial control of what content from the conversation was included in the book. Each student would also be able to choose a pseudonym if they wished. Finally, we asked each student to sign a consent form. We tried to make interviews seem as informal as possible. We had some standard questions, such as the previously mentioned "What is the first thing you believe others notice about you?" Our conversations typically lasted somewhere between twenty minutes and one hour, though, as might be expected, some students had more to say while others kept their responses brief. Pre-pandemic, all conversations were conducted in-person and were audio-recorded. During the pandemic, we had conversations with several people via Zoom. Once a conversation was concluded, we thanked the participant for their time and kept their contact information for follow-up questions as well as to obtain their official consent for portions of their narratives to be published.

Once all the conversations were complete, we had each audio recording transcribed by an IRB-approved service. At this point, we met collectively (including with our faculty advisor) to "code" the interviews – reading for possible similar themes and patterns across conversations. These themes became the basis for how we would order the materials in the book. Our sense was a theme-based focus would provide the most accurate representation of the collective insights of those who participated in the study. At first, we also thought the best way to represent those conversations was to delete all of our questions and then shape each transcript into a narrative that would flow as a story told from the point of view of the interviewee. There were two issues that arose with that initial decision. First, due to logistical and time constraints, we soon realized we could not possibly edit all 36 interviews into narratives. The book would never be finished and would be too long.

For that reason, we settled on a set of core narratives (approximately 16) which would ground the book. These core narratives would then be supplemented by small moments from our conversations that expanded or complicated an element of that core narrative. To put into basic terms, core narratives are the spine of the chapters of the book, while small moments supplement central points. (This will make more sense when you read the "Amplified Voices" section of this introduction.) Second, we decided to allow (as much as possible) for the student's full conversation to be represented in the core interviews. To this end, we did not edit the core narratives down to "one core theme," but allowed the full complexity of experience out of which that theme emerged to be represented. Some might find that this narrative complexity slows down their reading, but it is this very slow consideration of a Muslim student's experience which our project was attempting to achieve.

Discovered Possibilities

As this project neared completion, we asked ourselves, "What have we learned? What will others learn from engaging with the experiences of Muslim students at UVA?" In drawing such conclusions, we continually reminded ourselves that the majority of the interviews collected in this book were done between the months of April 2019-March 2020, before the pandemic had so profoundly affected the way students learn, socialize, and engage with the university. Since these interviews have occurred, academic departments have no doubt altered curriculum, added new faculty, and attempted to meet student needs due to (and beyond) the pandemic. It is possible that some of the concerns cited in this book are being (or have been) addressed.

Rather than edit out such concerns, we decided to leave these points in the book. Our thought was that while the particular example might have been resolved, often, the student was making a broader point about UVA culture. One way to understand Visibly (and Invisibly) Muslim on-Grounds is as a nuanced representation of Muslim student experiences just prior to the pandemic, at a particular moment in time, but speaking to a broader sense of UVA culture. (To clear up any confusion over competing statements in the interviews about a specific issue, we have included a brief timeline of events so the reader can place any one narrative within the moment of its occurrence and within the history of UVA responses to students' concerns.) One way to judge the progress of UVA administration, programs and faculty, then, is whether the concerns expressed by Muslim students have been addressed and, more generally, if UVA culture has expanded to fully welcome all students into its community.

As we consider the shape of this historical snapshot, we believe this project succeeded in representing the diversity of our Muslim student community, manifested through the unique identities, heritages, and practice of Islam. Muslim students' unique day-to-day experiences within Muslim spaces as well as UVA at large are also made legible in all their difficulties and aspirations. Their differing (yet often aligned) perspectives on UVA's engagement (or lack thereof) with the Muslim community and its needs become visible. We are also proud that this common theme of "Muslim life at UVA" is discussed through a kaleidoscope of specific examples, such as faculty comments to Muslim students, classroom lectures about Islam, and departmental curricular approaches to Islam. Muslim student life emerges through discussions of social events, student groups, and self-governance. These experiences occur within Greek Life, Muslim student organizations, Student Council, Residential and Housing Life, and other Contracted Independent Organizations (CIOs).

If it is not already clear, we want to be sure to state: In representing this diversity of viewpoints, this book is not attempting to ultimately define Islam or provide "the correct" interpretation of Islam. This is not a book on theology or Islamic law. It is an academic study about Muslim students and their experiences at a predominantly white institution. We urge the reader to keep in mind that the interviewees in this book are also not Islamic Scholars, but Muslim students who practice the faith (to whatever degree that they do). They speak of it based on their understanding of Islam and what it means to them. To that end, what they say should not and cannot be used as the end-all-be-all definition of Islam. As the students in this book demonstrate, there are different schools of thought within the faith. Each student has their own interpretation based on what to believe and practice. It is neither the goal nor the focus of this project to determine which is right or wrong, if any. For this reason, all understandings of the faith, as interpreted by each interviewee, were presented equally. If the reader is, however, wanting to know more on Islam's rulings regarding a topic of interest, we recommend consulting additional resources such as the Qur'an and the Hadith, as well as Islamic history written by Muslim scholars.

Instead of offering a "definition," then, we hoped to capture the continual mediation by Muslim students on what it means "to belong at UVA," often within concerns about their physical and emotional safety as well as the risks of disclosing their full identity on-Grounds and within Muslim spaces. Speaking as individuals, but reflecting a collective concern, the Muslim students in this book ask: is UVA really doing all it can to make Muslims feel safe and welcome at the institution? Do Muslim students feel supported? If not, does the responsibility for producing required changes rest with UVA or the Muslim students themselves? While we found that our Muslim peers' perspectives with regards to almost all of these topics are quite varied – some of them agreeing, others disagreeing – they all felt the urgency for a more robust university-wide discussion.

However, there were some perspectives that most, if not all, of our interviewees shared.

Given the framework of this project, Islam as a subject of study within academic classrooms was a shared focus across almost all our conversations. There was a tension between Muslim students' desire to have a clear understanding of Islam taught in classrooms and the various understandings of Islam represented by these very students. Students clearly recognized that any discussion of Islam was occurring within specific disciplinary contexts. For example, a Religious Studies course on the history of Islam would ask a different set of questions than a course on Women and Gender Studies. Students understood that any particular instructor's presentation of an issue was necessarily informed by their department's curriculum and mission, as well as their particular scholarly training. Students were not naive about these facts, nor were they arguing, ultimately, for a specific form of Islam to be enforced across all classrooms. Rather, they were making what might be an even more serious point: the very pedagogies used to teach about Islamic beliefs, histories, and communities too often placed Muslim students in difficult (and unnecessary) positions in the classroom. And to the extent professors are required to frame their course focus within disciplinary paradigms steeped in such frameworks, both professors and students are ill-served.

Indeed, many students noted how often discriminatory stereotypes brought into classroom discussion or inherent in assigned material were left unchallenged. As such, Muslim students were too often called upon to defend their faith as well as their culture. Even while recognizing the work of different academic fields, there was consensus that the pedagogies and methods within courses that took Islam as a topic of study too often served to perpetuate the misconceptions that exist about Islam. To that end, almost all the Muslims we interviewed were dissatisfied with some or all aspects of how they encountered Islam within their classes at UVA. Many decided to never take such a course in the first place. And while courses in some departments such as Global Studies or Religious Studies are cited by students, we do not want to create the impression this is an issue within a single or small set of departments. Nor should student opinions be understood as fully representing how and why a particular professor undertook teaching a particular course. Such a framing would take a historical snapshot by individual students as representing an inherent attribute of that department or faculty member. It would fail to consider recent faculty hires, as well as changes in curriculum made by departments since these interviews took place. It would mistake a particular professor or class as the solution point for a systemic issue across numerous classrooms, majors, and departments. Such a framing would relieve all other departments and faculty from considering how their classroom practices create environments hostile or threatening to Muslim students regardless of subject matter. In other words, that a particular department is not mentioned by students does not mean it is not part of the very same problems that our interviewees mention.

The majority of our conversations concerning UVA classrooms also ultimately ended on the opinion that all minority students at UVA, not just Muslim students, could benefit from having more faculty that shared said students' backgrounds. Muslim students expressed the strong belief that Muslim professors, deans, and administrators would understand their day-to-day struggles. The students would feel better supported and less alone. After all, it's human nature to feel comfort when seeing or being around others that share one's background and experiences. And here again, the call for more diversity among faculty, whether diversity is understood in terms of religious belief, race, class, gender, or sexuality is one that could apply to many departments within UVA. We also want to express our gratitude to the faculty who read the final manuscript, shared their input as well as support, and have already offered opportunities to meet with Muslim students, to learn more about their concerns. The actions of these faculty have already begun the process of creating the change hoped for by Muslim students.

To be clear, Muslim students also expressed their appreciation for friends, faculty, and organizations which actively worked to include their aspirations and concerns. If there are stories about faculty whose classes failed to address stereotypes, there are also stories of faculty apologizing for singling out Muslim students, and learning moments that turned into powerful mentoring relationships. If there are stories of Muslim students being attacked unfairly by a student leader, these are met with powerful testimonies about administrators who advocated and defended the right of Muslim students to be safe from verbal and physical harassment on Grounds. And across almost all the stories shared in this book, there are examples of individual students reaching out to support Muslim student identity, actively altering social plans to expand who could attend, and demanding that organizations change to better represent the complexity of the Muslim community. It would be unfair to the voices in this book to not highlight such moments of individual and collective kindnesses and acts of justice. And it would be equally unfair to imagine that kind responses from individuals in any way erase, mitigate, or lessen the personal pain caused by collective acts of bigotry.

Finally, there was one insight from this project worth noting: If Muslim students feel endlessly observed by the majority-white UVA student population, they are also observing the words and actions of that majority-white student community. The experiences of the Muslim students in this book are set in the context of the general student population's lens of Islamophobic bigotry, often perpetuated by poorly-informed media coverage and strengthened when courses are taught poorly. Which is to say, Islamophobia is not so much the "fault" of individual students, but the result of an echo-chamber that presents few alternatives to such bigotry. Indeed, this book shares numerous student stories – a powerful compilation – of years of being stereotyped, generalized, and systematically-boxed into a certain definition of "Muslim" by a culture of "whiteness" that doesn't represent who they truly are as real people. What this book provides is a lens for the reader to see how Muslim students understand this "whiteness" as a socially-constructed framework, instantiated by individuals, but supported by a myriad of curricular, administrative, and cultural frameworks. When spoken by the students in this book, the term "white" is not so much referring to an individual or to skin color, but to the entire creed of assumptions and the privileges that it affords, such as the ability to overpower conversations and be praised for it, the freedom to not have to code-switch depending on your audience, the liberty to commit a certain deed and not have it be attributed to your entire community, and the luxury to not have to constantly worry about whether your cultural and religious practices will make you a victim of a hate crime.

If when engaging with the voices of Muslim students, then, the reader finds himself/herself/themselves feeling misrepresented by such generalizations, feeling personally attacked by "unfair stereotypes," then the book has done its job in temporarily communicating the experience that Muslim students live through on a daily basis. One of the purposes of this book was to create a more nuanced understanding for non-Muslim students, and in doing so, hopefully break the cycle of misrecognition. Perhaps retaining the emotional response of having your individual life journey reduced to a stereotype, that feeling of injustice and shame, might ultimately be the origin point for a greater recognition of the complex humanity which resides in all of us – if, that is, we take time to listen.

Amplified Voices

It is difficult to capture in print the sense of recognition and shared understanding created during our conversations with the students in this collection. The release of energy, the intensity, and commitment which coursed through their personal stories acted as a connective tissue. A story about the work of a Muslim student to build more opportunities for his community drew strength from a memory of how a student navigated a hostile classroom environment. Moments marking the silencing of Muslim student concerns were understood in the context of increased representation in residential hall and student organization. In the process, some experiences were repeated but with different elements and different conclusions being drawn. Latent within this emerging tapestry was a sense that a space was opening up which might capture the reality, in all its nuance, of living as a Muslim student at UVA, in the South, in the United States, and in the early 21st century. It was a collective expression by a community that also demonstrated the importance of building a Grounds that is more open to the complexity of their experiences, more committed to allowing student culture to be enriched by a diversity of cultures, experiences, and heritages. It spoke of what "could be" in the face of "what is."

In structuring this book, we have attempted to represent how these collective voices grounded their conversations in a set of key experiences, then we consistently drew out the implications of such moments. For this reason, we have chosen three key terms as organizing principles of this collection: Classroom, Culture, Community. We devote one chapter to each of these three terms. Each chapter will open with a brief overview of the issues discussed. The chapter will then feature a few extended student narratives, where the key term is placed within the context of classrooms, social events, student organizations, and the local communities. Following each extended narrative, we provide shorter narratives where students further develop the conversation. Here the goal is not to provide solutions or to produce a restrictive definition of "Culture," for instance. Rather the goal is to represent how our community opens up different pathways for exploration and increased understanding. The chapters are an invitation to join this discussion, to ground our public dialogues in a different ethos of community.

Here we need to provide some additional background for one particular dialogue within the UVA Muslim student community. Throughout the book, but specifically in the last section of the book titled "Community", many of the interviewees refer to a letter that was sent to MSA from in-group members. To provide some context for the reader, we offer a brief synopsis of agreed upon facts about this event. Please bear in mind that this is a brief description of the events. We discussed only what we thought to be necessary for providing context; there is more to the events than will be mentioned in this brief summary, some of which are detailed by those interviewed in this book. We don't intend to persuade the reader of how to understand this event, but to give the reader enough details to understand the student's interpretation of that event.

In Spring of 2020, a letter addressed to the MSA Council was sent to the MSA at large. This letter detailed the years of frustrations that certain MSA members felt, particularly members whose identities was not as largely represented within the UVA MSA; these include but are not limited to Shia Muslims, Black Muslims, queer Muslims, members with varying levels of religiosity, and others. The letter charged MSA with being non-inclusive towards aforementioned minorities and, at times, even blind to certain insensitive actions/comments directed at those minorities. Moreover, it mentioned that the MSA was too often complacent with the majority's wishes at the expense of minorities in the name of preserving unity. The letter was signed by allies from within and outside of MSA. It listed changes that the MSA needed to make, both structurally and in its social engagements. If these demands weren't met, the letter stated, student members would be forced to leave and create new Muslim spaces that catered to their needs. Although the letter was addressed to the MSA council of that year, it was not necessarily a result of any one event that happened, but the culmination of years of frustrations, feelings of unwelcomeness, and feelings of non-belonging experienced by the authors and their respective communities. The MSA Council, as a response, held a town-hall meeting to listen to their members' concerns. Afterward, the Council drafted and sent out a formal response addressing the listed charges, concerns, and demands; highlighting the rich diversity that exists within the

Muslim community and the challenges that come with creating as well as managing a space for such a diverse group. To that end, the council's response included a full support and willingness to nurture any space that will be created for mentioned minorities. The establishment of the two Contracted Independent Organizations (CIOs), "Muslims United at UVA" and "Black Muslims at UVA", came about the following semester. Once established, the MSA tried to provide help and support to those spaces whenever possible, whilst making sure not to overstep boundaries.

Finally, we have also worked to ensure every student involved could determine how their voice is represented.For some students there was a personal desire to see their name in print. For others, their motivation was to publicly announce a political or cultural stance. Some students chose to use a pseudonym, which were generated by an online program which assigned random initials for an author. It would be too easy – but not entirely inaccurate – to assume this decision was based on concerns about personal safety or concerns about damaging their future careers. There is ample evidence in this collection of the risks and dangers associated with Muslim students taking a public stance or even just wearing a cultural marker of religious faith, such as the hijab. Within this context, we feel honored that students have entrusted us with their stories. We want to suggest, however, another reason for the decision to use a pseudonym. In any collection of personal testimonies, narratives, there is a natural inclination to ascribe the experiences expressed as unique to that individual. Yet clearly that is not the case for many of the experiences expressed in this collection. For that reason, we would argue that it is equally plausible to understand the student's choice to use a pseudonym as a way to mark the experience as common, systemic, needing more than just personal sympathy or support in response. We believe such an understanding will position the reader as having the responsibility to look at the structures which shape the stories and not use the personal experience as a way to be relieved of having to act, to respond to the collective experience represented in the following pages.

Final Thoughts

Wafa Salah: UVA's Diversity and Inclusion vision statement contains the following: "Inclusion goes beyond diversity, to recognize that people from diverse backgrounds must be truly included and participatory in order for their diversity to influence the community. Both diversity and inclusion are critical to our mission and they work best when they are an integral and celebrated part of our community." As I was reading this vision statement in full I was pleasantly surprised, for it was the most honest I have seen the university be in all my four years at the institution. The statement was in full admission of the school's tainted history with respect to supporting slavery and eugenics, its role in the stealing of tribal lands, the true purpose of UVA's establishment, and the exclusivity with which it operates still today. Additionally, the tone and diction coupled with how well it laid out the challenges of such an undertaking --making inclusive an institution that is exclusive by design-- made me believe that the university will be intentional and unrelenting in its pursuit of inclusion.

As I read the concluding statements, however, I couldn't help but feel lied to at the same time. I felt that what I read were just pretty words, designed to cajole me and those like me into thinking that the university is doing everything it can and should do to make itself inclusive. This part, in particular, undid everything, "We will settle for no less than a university. . . where community members are open and interested in learning about different backgrounds and perspectives, and where people feel physically and emotionally safe and have a strong sense of belonging." Although these are nice words to hear, how many minority students at UVA, in actuality, feel that this is true? How many would agree that their broader student community members are "open and interested" in learning about them? Do they truly feel "safe" and "have a strong sense of belonging" at the school? We would argue that the voices in this book testify that this inclusivity is no more than an unkept promise, an unlived reality.

Fawzia Tahsin: We are indebted and grateful that students have chosen to trust us with their experiences. We want to ensure their courage and their vulnerability in speaking will make a difference; that their voices will be part of an institutional effort to realize the goals in UVA's Diversity and Inclusion statement. As their voices start to circulate within and beyond UVA, then, we hope to see more accountability from faculty across academic departments on the concerns expressed in this book. Such accountability could be seen by having department committee meetings with the Muslim Students Association and other under-represented identities at UVA to ensure safe and productive classrooms for all students, as well as providing academic support when necessary. We would also hope to see the UVA administration be more accountable to the concerns expressed in this book. Such efforts might include active responses to physical or verbal attacks against Muslim students as well as holding student organizations accountable for Islamophobic actions. Lastly, we would hope to see a shift in the culture of UVA towards Muslim students. Such a cultural shift would result in increased allyship, as well as mental and emotional support, of Muslim students facing harassment or threats.

Wafa Salah: This book is not just for the Muslim student community. The issues raised concern everyone and anyone who is affiliated with the University of Virginia. As such, we ask that the reader of this book listen to the students' stories with the intent to understand, not to react in a defensive manner, but to truly gain insight on their perspective. No student did this interview with the intent of attacking any individual, group, community, faculty, department, or office. We ask you not to become preoccupied with any one detail and lose sight of the core issues being communicated. We also ask for your help in making sure this book is read earnestly, shared widely, and its concerns supported. And for our peers who understand how addressing the specific issues in this book improves the education of every student, we ask that you advocate for change, through any means, however large or small. Finally, especially those in positions of power, leadership, administration, and office, we ask that you be committed to the changes promised by the Diversity and Inclusion statement. Convince students you are sincere by keeping your public promises and not just make statements for the purpose of "checking boxes." Give these students and their stories the attention they merit. Address their concerns and those of other under-represented students with the sincerity and commitment that it deserves.

Fawzia Tahsin: Change does not happen overnight. But being complacent is not and should not be an option. Rather, change is about the slow work of doing better every day. It is about knowing when to do better and actually caring to do better. It is about finding the courage to speak up and speak out. Students don't speak out against UVA because they hate UVA. They speak out because they care about UVA. They are willing to criticize, speak out, and face backlash, so they can create a better university not only for future Muslim students and minority students, but for ALL students. They speak out of their love for UVA, for what it is and what it can become. They speak out to join the voices of students across the centuries that struggled to ensure UVA would never be complacent in its legacy but work endlessly to create a more inclusive and expansive future for all those who walk these Grounds.

Timeline of Relevant Events as Cited by UVA Student Participants

2016

October:
"Terrorist" is written on the door of the UVA dorm room of two Muslim students.

2017

August:
"Unite the Right Rally" occurs in Charlottesville, Virginia.

2018

August:
Jim Ryan becomes the 9th President of the University of Virginia.

2019

March:
Members of the Muslim student community request UVA administration makes a formal response to the Christchurch shooting in New Zealand.

2020

February:
Interfaith Student Center is opened at the University of Virginia.

The Muslim Student Association receives a letter expressing concerns about representation within the organization and initiates a response.

May:
Black Muslims at UVA and Muslims United at UVA become formal Contracted Independent Organizations at the University of Virginia.

CHAPTER ONE
Classrooms

Ayah Mahdi, Faris Musa, Palwasha Ayyub, F.C., Narjes Bencheikh, K.S., R.M., Javaria Abbasi, Noor Samee, Sara Ali, J.H., M.B., P.E., Isata Kamara, Fadumo Hussein, T.J., K.G., Y.H., M. Ahmad

Islam is a religion. But as the students in this chapter argue, at UVA, Islam is also an identity marker. And too often, Muslim identity is reduced to a series of symbols (think hijab), or inhumane practices (think terrorism). One result of such narrow conceptions of Islam, these students argue, is a form of social exclusion. Most student parties feature alcohol; students who practice Islam are not supposed to drink or be around alcohol. In this way, Muslim students are "Othered." And once "Othered," these cultural markers then seem to authorize verbal harassment, silencing, and threats of violence against Muslim students on-Grounds. In response, the students in this chapter invest the classroom with the possibility of producing a change in attitudes, beliefs, and, hopefully, actions. Yet too often, these same students find themselves struggling to enroll in classes where the pedagogy teaches the tenants of their faith or articulate its beliefs in a way that pushes against Islamophobic attitudes. Too often , the environment of classrooms focused on Islam envelope their voices within contexts that participate in the same stereotypes and distortions experienced on-Grounds. To address this situation, the students in this chapter suggest hiring more professors with deep knowledge of Islamic religious principles, with a focus on hiring practicing Muslims, if possible. They suggest the university might also support the faculty who work to create an atmosphere which rejects narrow frameworks in favor of nuanced engagement with Muslim students. End classroom discussions where Muslim students are made to represent or defend "Islam." Expand classrooms where their religious beliefs and cultural experiences enrichen student discussions. For ultimately, these students argue, UVA students are committed to understanding and supporting diverse religious practices and cultures at UVA. They simply need courses and professors who make that education possible.

MUSLIMS ARE NOT A MONOLITH

Ayah Mahdi
College of Arts and Sciences
Class of 2020

Ayah Mahdi's narrative initiates a conversation about the experience of being a student in classes focusing on Islam. She uses these experiences to highlight the disconnect between the Muslim student community and the wider UVA student body. Mahdi's insights are then expanded and commented upon by Muslim students at UVA who have concerns with the current pedagogy of Islamic classes, with some expressing the belief that such classes have become too Westernized. Taken together, our hope is these voices capture the nuances and complexities of bringing religious beliefs into an academic setting.

My first year, I had a really bad experience. I didn't feel comfortable. Nobody really wanted to talk to me because of my religion. It was the year that Trump was running for president, too. I lived in a predominantly pro-Trump environment, a hall full of Trump supporters, so I felt very isolated. I remember during my first year, I was walking back to my dorm and a group of white guys were just passing by me. One of them looked at me and he just spat at my feet. On top of the pro-Trump sentiments that a lot of my hallmates carried, people also definitely judged me because I wasn't into partying and drinking. So, I was totally made to feel like an outcast. People wouldn't really talk to me. They would laugh behind my back. It was just a very tough time for me because it was also my first year at UVA. I wanted to make friends with these people, but since I wasn't doing what they were doing, I didn't. It was tough.

I believe there's a disconnect between Muslims and the rest of the university. There is a very dominant white culture at UVA. They tend to subscribe to certain ways of thinking or acting. I don't know if it is due to their upbringing, but a lot of the white people on-Grounds don't really feel comfortable talking to Muslims such as myself. I say this because I'm visibly Muslim. I wear a hijab. Therefore, I guess people are very scared or hesitant to talk to me. They assume that I think in this type of way or that I act in a certain way. They don't really give me a chance to fully show who I am as a person. There's a wide range of people here. Some people are more conservative than others. By conservative, I mean western ideas of conservativism, so a lot of people don't agree with Islam or Muslims. I have heard things about people not really wanting to interact with Muslims, so there is an issue. This isn't my personal experience, but I've had friends who wear the hijab and they were attacked, not physically, but they've been harassed.

Media narratives about Islam are just so pervasive. People are going to take what they're being fed. Some people will seek out knowledge, but other people don't care. They just have these conceptions until you reach out to them. I do not believe, however, it should be a one-sided relationship. People need to seek out knowledge for themselves. They need to do their own research. I don't think it should be expected of me to explain my religion to those who misunderstand it. It shouldn't be only me making such an effort. People should reach out to me as well. Yes, I want to be there and have the conversation, but I want them to meet me halfway. We can come to an understanding. Still mere ignorance is a factor as well. People have a certain view of Islam, and some people don't want to do the research to learn differently, even though they know that it is not really all that black and white. Some people want to hold these perceptions of a misconstrued Islam and aren't willing to concede or change their views. In that sense, there is really not much that we Muslims can do.

I recently took my first Islam-related class. A lot of the information that the professor taught in that class goes completely against what I've been taught. I don't want to say that the professor is wrong and that I am right, but the professor was not really giving students a true sense of how Islam was practiced at that time and how it is practiced now. A lot of students take these kinds of classes to get a better sense of Islam, yet this professor was only feeding into the misunderstandings people already hold. For instance, he sent us an article about marriage. I believe it was an excerpt from a book that he had written. In the article, it says that your father is allowed to marry you off even if you're a minor. It says you have no say in the matter. In Islam, that is completely untrue! That piece of information in particular stuck out to me from the rest of the article because people see my hijab. They assume that I was forced to wear it. Granted, there are Muslim women out there who are forced to wear the hijab, but I think the majority of us were not forced to do so. That article just feeds into that narrative that Muslim women are docile, that they don't have any control over their lives, that the men are ruling over them. There might be instances where what he says might be the case, but those are just instances and not what Islam teaches. Muslim women have minds of their own. They can think, and they can take action for themselves.

Somebody later wrote a forum post for the class's discussion board regarding that reading. They were talking about how Muslim women are victims to the patriarchy of Islam. It was completely untrue! I understand that that student might have come into the class having that mistaken perception, but that student was not supposed to leave the class having that misconception confirmed, which is exactly what this article that the professor wrote did. I understand that it's a class based off of history, but at the same time, the professor didn't acknowledge or mention that such types of practices are not what Islam teaches today, not all Muslims engage in these practices. I feel like the students who took this class will look at me now and believe that I can't think for myself. That I have no control over my actions. That my hijab is just a sign of the patriarchy when it is not like that at all. This class was meant to be a class where I could talk about Islam, but that was not what I got.

I had a similar experience in a class on classical Islam. The professor would make very distasteful remarks that, for other people, may not be seen as an insult, but to me, as a Muslim, it was an insult. It was distasteful and I don't think it was required or acceptable in such a setting. I don't know if the university has done any research into the professor's teaching, but even if it did, I personally don't think the university would really do anything about it. UVA has this very "Free speech is everything" idea. I one hundred percent agree. Everybody should have freedom of speech, but I don't think it should be at the expense of other people. It should not be suppressing anybody's beliefs or religions. I've known of certain universities who have invited white supremacists to talk at their universities. White supremacists who are taunting and spouting all this rhetoric that's just hateful. Such acts, to me, are not okay. So there's this idea of free speech and that nothing can go against that idea, even if the university's own students feel uncomfortable in these classes, even if they feel insulted. And the way that these classes on Islam are being taught is just furthering that misconstrued insulting rhetoric. Then these students go out and further propagate that misinformation. It's pervasive, to be honest.

I try to speak up in classes and clarify points that I think are being misunderstood or not communicated at all, but sometimes what I say is not taken seriously or it's considered whining. For instance, I'm taking a class right now. It's not really a class on Islam, but it explains the point that I'm trying to make. Initially going into this class, I thought the class would be focused on only European travels, but we've really explored a lot that I didn't expect. We were talking about the word "exotic" and how it is problematic. The majority of my class is very white. In fact, other than me, there's only two other minorities. A lot of students in the class didn't really see an issue with that word, but I hated it. I would share my perspective and try to get them to see why minorities or mixed people, for example me, have an issue with this word. A lot of people would just follow up with something else and just completely gloss over my point. They would say things along the lines of, "Oh, I understand that, but I, personally, don't believe it." I'm just like, "Honey, we're not talking about 'I,' we're talking about a whole system!" I feel like people gloss over what I say, or they think, "Oh, here she goes again."

That is my experience. Their experience is just as important as mine. I want to hear what they have to say, but they also have to hear what I have to say. It should be a mutual exchange. It should be respectful. People should want to listen. I have my own views on many topics, for sure. I even have very staunch views sometimes, but I still like to hear how other people think. Sometimes, soft views can change, and those debates really fuel me. I really wish there was more of that at UVA, but I don't really think there is because a lot of people think the same here.

If UVA were to hire more faculty that are people of color, some of these western narratives could change or shift. I don't want to generalize, but I feel like a lot of the white professors here at UVA tend to think or have very similar viewpoints. Bringing in people who think in a different way, I believe, would contribute to the solution. In America, a minority and a white person have completely different experiences, even if they're living in the same city, based on how society is structured as well as how people view a minority versus a white person. Therefore, minority teachers will definitely have viewpoints and experiences that a white professor would be unable to share. Furthermore, students coming into UVA would feel more comfortable, too, by having these figures of authority, somebody who looks like us and potentially understands how we've lived and what we've experienced I believe would definitely make UVA a lot more comfortable. Minority students would have someone to go to and share their experiences.

I have mentioned several times now that I am visibly Muslim. The first thing that people notice about me is my hijab. As a result, I feel that my hijab is all that my peers see; unless of course they've had experience with Muslims, but a lot of people here at UVA have not. I love the fact that I wear a hijab and I love that it defines me. At the same time though, it's a double-edged sword because people think that that is all I am, that I don't have any other aspects to my personality other than my religion, but that's not true whatsoever. I have aspirations; I have dreams; I have hobbies that don't necessarily ascribe to the western stereotypical female Muslim. I think that that perception holds them back from really getting to know me. They have this idea of what I am. They think that they would never get along with somebody who's so religious. I feel like people really don't make an effort to see that part of me. They paint me as just a Muslim girl. That we won't get along. I find it sad honestly because I love my religion, but I don't want that to be the only thing that people see me as.

In a different but similar sense, professors think the same way. They think that I have certain viewpoints that only align with what Islam believes. Islam is very diverse. Sometimes I have conflicting viewpoints, and for other people, sometimes they have conflicting viewpoints with me. A lot of people try not to offend me. I understand that it comes from a good place, but at the same time I think these discussions are needed. I feel bad saying it, but I want controversy! I want to have these discussions, theoretical debates, where I could give my viewpoint in class and then the professor could give their viewpoint, but in a respectful setting, of course. I don't want any hateful speech. I just don't like how people completely write off my thoughts or beliefs. I hate people just assume that I only believe in what Islam says. And I do, but at the same time, there's more to me. I'm more than just my religion.

Faris Musa
Class of 2020
McIntire School of Commerce

The way that Religious Studies courses are given here at UVA, it's as if you're treating Islam like it's a cadaver that you can dissect, it's some sort of dead thing. Islam is a *living* thing. And the nomenclature of "Religious Studies" is false in my opinion. What they teach in Religious Studies is a mutation of history with a combination of just a little bit of theology and any other cultural, anthropological, social psychology that they can mix in to teach a course. They are very open and honest about this being their department focus. But I feel if you really want to teach a class on any religion, the main focus, the crux of that course, should be about theology because you can't necessarily correlate the actions of a group of people and call that the religion. A very modern example could be Islam and ISIS, even though I really don't want to go into that, though. Other very common examples are the Crusades or the conquering of Jerusalem by the Muslims. My main point is that the actions of people do not equal the religion. Nonetheless, Religious Studies courses at UVA tend to focus so much on the individual, on cultures, on groups of people, on certain time periods, then analyze the actions of those people and then say that "is" the religion, in our case, Islam.

I also truly believe that there's some misinformation being spread in those types of courses. Especially when you're not going to focus on theology or doctrine but, instead, you focus on historical, cultural, anthropological contexts. One could argue that the religious courses here even support the misconceptions people already have coming into class. For example, if it is said in a class, "Muslims can have multiple wives," but the theology behind it is not discussed, then the misconception that women are not treated fairly in Islam is further propagated. Yes, we can have up to four wives, but there are limits even with that practice. You need to be able to support all your wives equally, both emotionally and financially. There are other components, but let's take those two, emotionally and financially. You need to treat both, all three or all four, of your wives, financially and emotionally equal. That, however, is almost impossible to do for any man if you want to talk about psychology and other studies that have been conducted. If, however, a student sees and learns that "Islam allows four wives" in a class, that student will be like, "Oh, the Muslims could just have multiple wives. Sounds like a religion that doesn't necessarily treat women as fairly." As a result, those misconceptions get piled up, reinforced, and solidified within the individual as well as society.

From my perspective, the Religious Studies department, with their historical focus, absolutely does not do justice to Islamic theology. None at all. Moreover, I feel like there's a very simple solution. You get someone who practices the religion and is a scholar in that religion to teach the religion. You don't get a Harvard Ph.D. whose thesis was on one little branch of Islam looking at how it impacted cultural practices of media and art. Sure, there can be cultural impacts produced by Islam, but that does not necessarily have anything to do with theological doctrine. It has absolutely nothing to do with theology if you want to be real.

Palwasha Ayyub
Class of 2023
College of Arts and Sciences

When studying classical Islam, I found myself focusing more on dates and textbook history, instead of learning more about how some Islamic principles apply in everyday life. I guess that applies to the class's curriculum, because it discusses different accomplishments of Islam over the years in a sequential manner. There isn't much room for your own thought in the course, though. I couldn't voice my opinion without being questioned or completely dismissed by the professor, which I noticed has happened to some students. They will make a comment and the professor will respond, "Well, that's just ... Well, that's not what it is." I don't know why he does that. I can't tell if he tries to keep the class very objective or unbiased because there's a lot of Muslims in the class. If so, maybe he didn't want to incorporate that much thought or opinion since this would change the structure of the class. I agree that being unbiased is important in teaching settings, but I feel like there should also be room to interpret things instead of just memorizing things from a textbook.

I'm also taking courses in Women and Gender Studies (WGS) this semester. I believe that all WGS classes should have some sense of empowerment in them because they're discussing such important topics. I was always curious about the role of women in Islam. Growing up in America, I've noticed how being Muslim is interpreted. When I go back to where my parents grew up, the role of women is so different over there. When I took this class, I expected a lot of discussion about how the role of women is different in different places. I was expecting we would be discussing and deconstructing barriers that prohibit women from becoming active and well-integrated members of society. But for that class, we just talk about dates. We just talk about textbook history, like my course on classical Islam. Although you can voice your opinions, the professor doesn't take opinions that well. If you have something specific to say from a textbook or a reading, if you have some specific point to elaborate on, that's all she will listen to. If you interpret something in a different way, she doesn't exactly understand varying perspectives. I think that may be an attempt at being non-biased or just being objective again. I get that, but I think you should have space in these classrooms to talk about Islam in relation to your own individual self. Such space is important. It should be unbiased, but if there is not much room to voice your own interpretations, I think that's definitely a problem.

F.C.

I've taken courses at UVA about classical Islam. Oftentimes, the teacher was not Muslim and, therefore, had his own kind of biases toward the subject that stemmed from his own beliefs about the religion. The content was fine, but obviously having teachers that are not Muslim, or teachers that are not a complete expert in the field, makes you feel that Islam is being represented inaccurately, from a different lens that is not entirely accurate. But in general, Islam, it feels like it has a place here at UVA.

Even though the Islam-related courses that I've taken were not covering a major requirement, I was interested in taking those classes to better educate myself. I wanted to understand how the West interprets Islam as well as how people from other religions view it. For instance, Islam in the Middle East and within other Muslim countries is a lot different than here. Islam has been in that region for a much longer time. But the Western perspective is different from the Middle Eastern because Islam is viewed as a new thing, even though it's not. Also, since Islam has been growing lately in the United States, some people have kind of developed these wrong beliefs and images regarding Islam based on ISIS and different terrorist organizations. That influences the perception of Islam by the students at UVA. Over time, you also can see that some professors have mixed views about Islam from their original biases and the biases that are taught to them by academia.

Overall, though, these courses felt fine. I'm taking a class this semester that brought up Islam. The professor brought an actual Muslim guest speaker to speak about Islam. He did a really good job explaining himself and his point of view as well as representing it accurately, which is something that I really liked. But then, in a class on classical Islam, the teaching was different. The teacher had his own views and bias about Islam which influenced the way he taught the class. Even people from this current and past semester stated that he would mention the history written by Islam is not exactly accurate because there were not any other people who wrote it down. It was only Muslims who wrote down their history, so it might have been different. That means that Islam is not accurate. Everything is false because history has been "manipulated" by the Muslims who wrote it. People were conflicted about that point, including me.

In general, though, I feel like Islam's represented in a good way. The guest speaker that came to our class was actually a Muslim as well as being Indian. I think this shows that having more faculty like him who represent different cultures, ethnicities, and religions can be really helpful to the UVA faculty, especially when UVA faculty is white-dominant. There isn't a lot of representation for those different backgrounds and ethnicities, specifically in classes. So having more diverse faculty will ensure that teachers will be able to deliver a message consistent with what they believe in and have the experience to make the class more engaging and fun.

Narjes Bencheikh
Class of 2020
College of Arts and Sciences

I've never taken a class specifically on Islam because I was always told by up-perclassmen to avoid them. Most of them are taught by white professors, and it's never going to end well. Still, I just always heard bad things so I just always avoided it. I'm not in a major where it's required to take religion classes. I've always just focused more so on the Middle East, the Arab side of things versus the Islamic side. If I didn't have friends telling me to avoid taking the courses, I probably would have taken some. I know at one point I had "Islam in Africa" in my shopping cart, but I just have never gone through with it. I know this semester there are some courses where they are taught by non-white professors.

I think having more faculty of color is important. I had a statistics professor that was African American and then my Arabic professors are Arab. But other than that, I've only been taught by white professors. Especially for global public health, all the professors being white does not give you a global perspective. This professor draws all her global experiences from two years she spent abroad. There was this one instance when the professor talked about Africa. Well, first of all, she talks about Africa as if it is one country, which already pisses me off. It's a whole continent. Anytime she talks about "Africa," she'll have these random jabs at Islam. At one point she said, "The Gambia," then made it a point to emphasize that it is a Muslim country, before telling us a story about how the men always had to eat first. Then whatever was left, like the scraps, the women would then go in and eat.

Nowhere in the Quran does it say that men need to go first and then whatever the scraps are, the women are eating. But she just kept emphasizing it. That's such a negative story reflecting the country and a Muslim country. Students that are, like, not paying attention are just going to associate women's inequality with Islam. Students deserve a perspective that isn't based on a white woman's perspective of going into a sub-Saharan African country for two years. I just feel like we have so much more to learn from diverse experiences. UVA's not doing a good job of delivering that.

K.S.

I generally avoid taking Islamic classes because I don't want to feel discomfort if the professor teaches it in a way that I don't believe is true. I am completely for people learning about Islam, but I don't think the classroom is necessarily a way to be introduced to Islam. One of my engagement classes for the new college curriculum was about Islam, and it was a very negative experience for me. I was in a discussion with someone who had taken the class in a previous time period. They were talking about how much they learned about Islam. I couldn't help but shake my head because what the professor was teaching was not Islam. It was maybe some historical form of Islam. But to me, it wasn't the Islam that I practice and believe in.

I only have my opinion of one specific professor. I've heard that other professors teach about Islam in a very good way, but I can't speak to their teaching personally. My professor presented it like, "Oh this is Islamism. It's not Islam." But the way the students were receiving the information was *as if it was* Islam, and that was the problem. I also had a problem with that professor, or rather, they had a problem with me. I felt continuously ignored. I would raise my hand, and they wouldn't call on me. I'd be talking, and they would cut me off. I would disagree with the professor and be shot down. I wasn't going to take an Islamic class in the first place. I decided to just try it out, and I've generally avoided them from then on.

I think the professor claimed to be Muslim. Maybe that made the professor feel like he could talk about all of Islam without bringing in other perspectives. I vehemently disagreed with that. I think that even whether you're Muslim or not, you should be able to teach the basics of Islam. It shouldn't be from a negative standpoint every single time. You can bring in issues that Muslims face today. You can bring in things that Muslims have to deal with or are fighting against. But to come in with the one perspective of "This is the hypocrisy of Islam" or "This is why all these people who said they were Muslim became terrorists"" that kind of thing, I think just brings in a really negative connotation to Islam that people don't need encouraged in this country. I think people need to actually meet Muslims who are actually practicing Islam in their daily lives. A lot of people don't meet Muslims until later in their lives when they've already had ample time to form prejudice. Some people never meet a Muslim in their 12 years of schooling, maybe until they're in the workforce. So having that kind of exposure that's inherently negative, it's just so harmful to our image.

R.M.

When you have to read academic writing on religion, it's taught in a way where I don't know how to describe it. They make it too academic. It gets skewed from the real meaning of Islam. Instead of using the Quran, they use some academic scholar to about Sufism and other historical parts of Islam. They approach it from a very PhD-like Western narrative of Islam. They translate Islam within their lectures to something else, then people who have no exposure to Islam take this variation as the true meaning of the religion. They'll spend two, three lectures on a really small part of the religion and make it seem a lot more important than it actually is. I don't know why it's taught this way. I think because there are PhD scholars that teach the class, like they have their PhD in this kind of stuff, so they are just taught to look at a religion from a different way and use all these other sources. But the true meaning is lost.

I think the best way that you can teach Islam is through the Quran. Any other source of trying to teach religion, outside of the Holy Book, is just someone's interpretation or academic research into the religion. The best way to learn the religion is through the Holy Book itself. I don't think that teaching what the religion is from the Quran is going to cause the professor to be biased. That's literally just teaching you the religion. It doesn't make the professor subjective towards it. They're not trying to convert you or anything. If they said statements like, "Oh, Islam is great. Islam is blah, blah, blah," then that's imposing their own opinions and their own beliefs. But if they just teach, "Oh, this is what the Quran says," or, "This is what Muslims do," then I don't think that there is anything wrong with that.

Javaria Abbasi
Class of 2020
College of Arts and Sciences

I have taken some classes in the Middle Eastern South Asian (MESA) department, one of which was on the Arab Spring. I absolutely hated that class mostly because the majority of the people enrolled in it were also ROTC students who were learning Arabic but had very pejorative views or provincial views of Islam that made me uncomfortable. I often felt as the hijabi in the class, I was looked at as having *to* defend indefensible things that people did in the name of my religion. But I didn't think that I should have to defend these actions because I don't agree with them.

I think the professor was a romantic in the sense that he was very infatuated with a certain era of Iranian Shia history. But I don't think he was problematic. I just think he had a very romantic picture of Islam generally. He was very interested in the ideals of the religion, but not so much in how they were practiced. And I think that this is true of, whether he was talking about Sunni Islam or Shia Islam, he was very much, "This is what Shia Islam *says*" Or "This is what Sunni Islam *says*. Therefore, "This is how people act." I think there's often, at any discussion, a distinction between what people believe and how they act. But he didn't seem willing to acknowledge, i.e., the idea that someone can believe something, still be a hypocrite, and do something problematic. It didn't really come up. I didn't find this all that problematic because I think that this is true with a lot of professors who teach, whether it's theology or philosophy. I don't think he was unique to his discussion of *Islam*.

It's not that I don't think Islam should be discussed academically. I definitely think it should be, but I think that a class on Islam in our recent political climate is really made or broken by the people in the class because sometimes even if the professor has the best intentions and articulates things the best way possible, people in class will interpret it as they wish based on their own political leanings, their own backgrounds. And I remember taking this class during Trump's election and it was contentious, to say the least.

"I HAVE ALWAYS BEEN BOTH THE STUDENT AND THE TEACHER"

Noor Samee
Class of 2021
College of Arts and Sciences

Noor Samee's narrative initiates a conversation on the experience of being a Muslim minority student in a majority-white classroom. She discusses the necessity of having to become a "teacher" in the class about her religion, rather than just a student there to learn from her professor and her peers. She misses learning from her peers and the value it adds to her education. Samee's insights are then expanded upon by Muslim students at UVA, who expand on the difficulties of being a minority in the classroom and highlight the need to find allyship with UVA professors.

I don't think that the Muslim presence is massive here at UVA. I think the majority is Christian or secular. A lot of the UVA community doesn't even talk about Islam in their everyday discourse and interactions. Frankly, I don't think that UVA is paying attention or valuing Muslim voices as much as they should. If I were to compare UVA to Virginia Commonwealth University (VCU), I don't think my experiences are that similar. Some things are similar. My experience in classrooms has been similar. I also had some racist teachers at VCU. But the social scene created a support system that allowed me to still be okay. Whereas here, I don't feel very supported. When I go through things, I don't feel like there's anyone that will genuinely advocate for me, genuinely support me, when a teacher is being racist. That's very different. It creates a lot more instability and insecurity for me. I don't feel like there's anything to fall back on if something goes wrong. I don't feel like if I have a complaint that has to do with racism or with Islamophobia, that it will genuinely be heard.

There was one experience that really confirmed every anxiety that I had about coming to UVA. In one class, our teacher was talking about museums in France and how they used to be racist. I raised my hand and said, "In future classes are we going to be talking about museums in the Middle East, in South Asia, in North Africa, the regions that we're supposed to be studying? Because the framing around France feels pretty colonialist to me." She did not like that question and decided to pull me out in the middle of class. She said, "I work really hard in this class, and you might not realize it, but I also put a lot of work into this class." I said, "I'm sure you do." She said, "If you didn't like this class, you should have just dropped." I said, "Well, I need this for my major. This is required." I added, "I have felt, in my experience of this classroom, that we are centering white people. And we are centering their surprise around racism. When, in my lived experiences as a person of color, racism is a reality. And racism is not something that I need to learn in a classroom. It's something that I've experienced from the time I was five years old. So, can we please move past this? Because, honestly, it is hindering my learning, and I deserve to learn just as much as everybody else."

She told me I need to wait until graduate school. That I should bring in my own experience and my own knowledge into the classroom and teach other students. When I talked to my advisor, she said the same thing. That was very frustrating for me because I have always been both the student and the teacher in these situations. I don't feel like that's my responsibility. I want to be able to sit back and genuinely learn something. I'm not an expert in the Middle East or South Asia or North Africa. I don't know anything about those regions, but I still felt like what we were covering was so basic.

One thing I took for granted at VCU was the value in learning from the people in your classroom, not necessarily just the teacher. When I came to UVA and I saw there were a lot of white people, a lot of non-Muslims, I realized I was not learning as much from the discussion. When I used to have discussions in my old classes, there would just be so many different experiences that would be raised, so many different opinions. They really enriched my learning, whereas, here, a lot of times, I'm the only Muslim in the room or the only Muslim that's speaking in the room. I didn't think about that when I was applying to UVA. But when I got to UVA, I realized that the classroom discussion would not be as rich. That wasn't a factor that I had considered. I considered a lot of factors. I knew that it was not going to be nearly as diverse, but I didn't think about how that would affect the classroom until I got here.

How to solve it? I would say enroll more people of color. I would also say hire more teachers of color. Even more than the student body being diverse, a lot of colleges don't recognize how important it is to have people of color as faculty. That might be more important because faculty are the ones that are shaping the minds of the students. They're the ones that are really leading and creating this university's academic culture. Students create social culture, but students can also find social pockets outside of the university if they need to. They can find social pockets within the vastness of the university. If they don't have teachers that are genuinely teaching them what they should be knowing about the world, however, they're going to have been poorly served by the university.

Students are also poorly served by UVA's "overbooking culture." I see a lot of people being very involved in particular organizations that are very exclusive and don't mingle with other groups. It's actually really funny because when I was at VCU, there was nothing like this. There were no applications for clubs. I had never heard of that before. At VCU, you just join a club and have fun. You put in as much energy as you are committed to the club, how much you actually care about it. Whereas at UVA, clubs are like jobs. It's just weird.

I've also noticed that things are very bureaucratic, there's so many hoops to jump through to get things done. Oftentimes, the people in power create hoops for organizations to jump through that lead them to no destination, resulting in the groups' members' interests falling into oblivion. It's always under the realm of, "Oh, this is just how the bureaucracy works. This is just how the system works. You have to do these certain things." I think it's a way of gatekeeping for sure. And creating all of these hoops to jump through for every single thing we need to do here is creating an inaccessible culture. It is creating a hyper-competitive culture around things that don't have competition in the real world. This competition is all created. It's not real. I think there does not need to be as much rigid frameworks, paperwork, boxes around everything that we do. I think it's okay for things to be a little bit messy, a little bit malleable. That's fine. I've seen it work. It does work.

But everyone I've met around here is just constantly over-booking themselves. I think that's one thing that I am very against. Growing up "overbooking" was my understanding of the world. I thought that you had to work yourself to death and that you had to treat your own body like a robot in order to be a successful or happy person. It took me going to VCU and being in a more relaxed environment to realize how wrong I was. In my experience at VCU, I started taking fewer classes, started taking classes later just to accommodate for the fact that I wanted to stay up late. It wasn't like I had to, but I wanted to. I wanted to cater to my comfort, and that's okay. That is completely okay. I think a lot of people here don't realize how important it is to just let yourself be relaxed.

There have been things that I've said "no" to that maybe I would have enjoyed, but life is long. I can do those things later. That's one thing that I'm really trying to stick to at UVA. I don't see a lot of people genuinely just following their passions, really exploring what's within them, what's driving them towards excitement and love and joy. I see a lot of people who do things because they think it will give them success, because they think it will be a good addition to their resume, because they think it'll make them fit in, all of those kinds of things, which is not the way I hope to live my life. I really hope I don't waver from it. I hope I don't get sucked into rigidity and competitiveness because that's not me. That's not healthy. It's been hard because there is a lot of pressure to do a lot of things, but I have been pretty firm.

I think my whole life, it's been a blessing and a curse that I have stayed very true to who I am. Definitely sometimes it's been quite a curse, because I was never comfortable with assimilating. I never wanted to do it. For me, the thing that's most important to me within my Islam and within my personality is honesty and transparency. Part of that is being my fullest self as much as I can be within every environment that I'm in. I think that I'm the same person in every environment, but also every environment will call for a different side of me. I felt pressure to be different at UVA for sure. I wouldn't say that I very easily can be my fullest self here, I can't. But I always work on trying to make sure that I am my fullest self within this environment.

Sara Ali
Class of 2021
College of Arts and Sciences
Class of 2022
McIntire School of Commerce

I was taking this one class. I won't name the professor because I have a great relationship with him now. But I was taking this class where we were talking about, I believe, the "culture assimilation machine." Essentially, we were talking about different cultures around the world and how once everyone migrates to America, we all become one mold. Then professor goes, "Look at all of you guys in class right now." (We're in Wilson 402, the biggest lecture room that I personally know of at UVA.) He goes, "Look, you're all dressed alike. Girls, most of you guys are in jeans, skinny jeans, khakis, Converse, Adidas." He's naming basic outfits, basic clothes, basic hoodies, shirts, Abercrombie & Fitch, naming the most basic brands. He goes "Everyone here is dressed alike." He's getting ready to continue, but then he stopped and looked at me. He's like, "Well, except you. You still kept your culture. You still wear your scarf." I was just in shock because he singled me out in front of around 200, maybe 300, students. Then he noticed how shocked I was about his statement. Instantly, my eyes flooded with water. I wouldn't say tears because I didn't want to cry in front of everyone. I was sitting in the third row from the front. So granted 90% of the class probably couldn't see me, but I was still very embarrassed because most people could see he was talking about me, calling me out saying, "Oh, you're just not like the rest of us." Then he backtracked because he realized his mistake. He saw the water in my eyes. So, he said, "Well yeah, you're still wearing skinny jeans. You're still wearing Converse, but you still kept your identity," That's when I felt, "Wow, my identity really singles me out sometimes." Sometimes I forget about that, how sometimes, I'm the only hijabi in my class, you know what I mean? It's something you forget because you get so used to it. Then someone mentions it, and you're like, "Oh, I am different," which isn't a good feeling. You want to be just like your peers. You want to just fit in. It's hard to do that when you're reminded constantly by others that you're not like them. And there is a certain degree to which that statement is true. I am not like them. I *do* wear the hijab. I *do* have a different religion. But I am like them in so many other aspects. We do share the same grade. We share the same work ethic. We're here at UVA together.

J.H.

I'm taking an anthropology class called "Multiculturalism, Racism, and Nationalism." It's been a very interesting class. My professor likes to go on tangents. When he does that, he likes to use students in his class to further support his arguments and to ask people if they have different perspectives and what not. I'm the only hijabi in my class, so I've been called on multiple times to talk about something that he mentioned. Sometimes, in the middle of class, he completely catches me by surprise where he's like, "Hey, you're hijabi. You can visibly be identified as an "Other," as a Muslim, as somebody who is not a Christian. How has that affected you?" He is basically asking about my personal experiences. Oftentimes I've had to say something and it's interesting, I really love it. I love being able to provide my own perspective in classes and being given an opportunity by the teacher to talk about something. I don't feel uncomfortable at all when a teacher wants to discuss something about me.

Of course, there was a review written on the course forum about our semester, and it was about me. Basically, the person, whoever it was, was saying that "The one thing I didn't like about the teacher was how they asked for students' perspectives," and in parentheses was written "hijab of Arab background." That student believed that the teacher should have used celebrities or famous people as examples. But the teacher's method made students share their perspectives. It was a way of reminding minorities of the different ways they're treated in a white society, the different ways they think about issues. I was like, "You are completely wrong because it makes us feel empowered when we get the opportunity to talk." I remember walking out and feeling so good that a teacher would ask me, in a class with 50 other students, what's it like to wear a hijab on-Grounds, you know? But, like, white students that live in a carefree world, most of them, they've never faced racial tension, racial hatred from people, mistreatment. Sometimes the best thing these students can do is to stop *you* from talking so that *they* could be saved from being reminded *we* have been treated as if we have lower status, that we have been treated that way. They want you to move on, but how are you going to move on if you don't talk about what's affecting you? So, I want to talk about what it's like to be a hijabi on-Grounds.

M.B.

In my first semester, I took a course on modern Islam. The class wasn't particularly enlightening in any way. I kind of just got through it. On the very last day, we finally got to modern Islam and about the topic of terrorism in the world, Muslim terrorism. To me, what I didn't appreciate, was that it was at this moment that my classmates were the most engaged, that what they wanted to hear the most about was terrorism, Muslim terrorism. "How does Islam relate to terrorism?" For me, when you have this entire class discussing the history, the modern apparatus, the system, everything to do with Muslim-Americans, Muslims overseas, all of that, it was not my favorite moment that the class about terrorism was the one about which people got the most excited. I understood it at the same time, but that moment didn't help with my feeling included by certain people, especially within the Religious Studies and Middle Eastern departments.

My other experience with the Middle Eastern Department was a class focused on Middle Eastern and Islamic history as well as colonialism. There were not a lot of Muslim, Arab, Desi, et cetera, students in class. The class was mostly white students. I don't recall any more than the types of things they were saying in class discussion, but it made me so frustrated at the depth of ignorance related to the topic. I ended up leaving the class a few minutes early and dropped it immediately. Even if the professor was open-minded and cultured and experienced in the subject, I don't think I could have lasted the entire semester dealing with people that ignorant. For example, we were talking about when Britain occupied India and Palestine. Britain completely overtook India and Palestine's education system to implement a Western system of education, and how damaging that was to the local culture, the local religion when their own language wasn't prioritized! Yet a couple of students raised their hands and were like, "I'm confused. Isn't it better for them to be learning English and learning Christianity and learning Western values? I don't see how it's damaging at all for other countries to be forced to learn the American or British education system." So, that among a couple of other comments, made me not excited about taking that class.

Javaria Abbasi
Class of 2020
College of Arts and Sciences

I think that being a hijabi and also being six foot three inches tall makes me very visible. Whether I want to or not, my actions are interpreted as the actions of capital "I" Islamic or a capital "M" Muslim. I think that I'm always hyper-cognizant of that at UVA. Perhaps the reason I am more hyperaware here at UVA than compared to high school is because the demographics are much more white here at UVA. I think that, in this sense, people might not encounter as many Muslims in their everyday life.

I am a Spanish and Political & Social Thought double major. In my Spanish classes, my identity as a Muslim woman doesn't come up, even when we are engaging in discussions of Islam. That can be refreshing because when we are talking about being Muslim in Latin America historically, for instance, I don't feel pressured to answer a certain way or perform in a certain way. I can answer just like any other student, even though it is a discussion about my religion. However, I find that in my politics classes, my hijab makes me a little bit more of a spectacle when we are discussing issues of Islam or religious terrorism. For instance, in my "Political and Social Thought" class, students read *Home Fire* by Kamila Shamsie. *Home Fire* is a modern-day retelling of Sophocles' *Antigone* as the narrative of a girl who wants to bury her brother who had joined ISIS. I found that in that class discussion, and many class discussions of my religion, people would look at me even when I wasn't speaking or stare at me a lot more in class in ways that sometimes made me very uncomfortable. But generally, I don't think that UVA's atmosphere is all that different from the rest of the public atmosphere in Virginia. I don't find that it's especially worse or especially better. I think a lot of it is just a reproduction of what I've seen in high school and middle school.

I do wish my classes talked more about cultural language differences. My family blends between Urdu and English unconsciously all the time. I think that there's an implicit understanding at UVA, however, about speaking standard English. If you do linguistics, it's almost a monoglot type standard. This standard can harm students who come from backgrounds in which they do code-switch at home very fluidly without thinking about it. I think that also can affect how fast you speak. It can affect your intonation. It can affect a lot of things. So, I do get a little annoyed when professors tell me to either slow down, don't speak so fast, or articulate a certain way. I know that such a standard is just constructed. Having done debate, where I engaged in so many different styles, I'm aware that there's not one standard for what sounds professional or what sounds persuasive.

I do get frustrated that we don't really train our professors with how to engage with students, especially in seminar discussion classes, who do come from different linguistic backgrounds. I know students for whom English is the third or fourth language which they speak. In my sorority, I have a ton of international sisters from East Asia. They often feel incredibly uncomfortable in discussion classes. They believe that even though their point is correct, their content is on point, that they are being judged for how they present it. It's unfair. It's not their first language. It might even be their fourth, in some cases. Professors will call them out on it. They will say, "Get to the point." Sometimes, though, they really have to take a little longer. I think that's something that UVA has to do better because I think diversity also has to encompass multilingual communities.

Narjes Bencheikh
Class of 2020
College of Arts and Sciences

I have friends at more diverse schools like Virginia Commonwealth University (VCU) or University of Maryland. When comparing UVA to those other colleges, my friends' experiences are a lot different. I think UVA is relatively inclusive, but VCU schools are *very* inclusive. VCU students have a lot more people that look like them than here at UVA. You'll be sitting in a UVA classroom, and you'll look around and realize that there's literally no one that looks like you. You know what I mean? With other schools, they have people of color. They have Muslims all around them. In classes at UVA where the professor will say something wrong about Islam or insinuate something wrong, I feel the burden to have to correct them, but I don't think that should be the case. When you're that one Muslim girl in the class, that burden does fall on you. In other schools, where there's more professors of diverse backgrounds, professors of color and more diverse students within the class, the burden doesn't fall on that one person. I feel like it alleviates some of that pressure. Whereas for us at UVA, it's very pronounced.

Sometimes in class discussions, when I am the only person of color in the room, the way I articulate my thoughts definitely makes me stand out in a predominantly white setting. It's hard not to stand out because my perspective is definitely going to be a lot different than anyone else's. In a sense, again, you are representing a whole faith whether you want to or not, but it's not always fun to have to defend your religion. In a class where you'd expect people to be open-minded, some people can just be like, "Oh, you're just being defensive." A lot of what I have to say can be misconstrued. They're not really willing to hear you out. Of course, you're going to defend your religion. You believe in it. As long as you present facts, though, I feel like it's kind of hard to argue back. Still, it's always a burden having to explain yourself. It gets exhausting. This could just be the general culture of UVA, a result of it not promoting more diverse classrooms.

P.E.

I've only had white professors so far at UVA. It's always been, "Oh the brown girl." I remember the first day of my Engagement class. Since most of my classes are lectures, I don't really talk to my professors. My Engagement class, though, is really small. I remember we were introducing ourselves with icebreakers. One question was, "What is the thing that you like most about UVA and one thing you don't like about UVA?" It came to me. I said, "I don't like that UVA is just not diverse." I said this to the whole class. There were only 15 people in the class. I think my teacher was like, "Oh, you're that kind of person who cares about diversity and inclusion." Since then, all my classmates seem to think that I'm the girl "who talks about diversity" and "talks about the Enslaved Laborers all the time" and "talks about the social justice stuff." My teachers notice that I'm very outspoken. I am a minority and I want to voice that fact and empower other people who are also minorities. In fact, my professor was really nice. I think most of the professors are really nice and open. I don't think it was taken badly by the professor. I just think she was not expecting it at first and thought, "Oh well, you're not like everyone else."

Isata Kamara
Class of 2022
College of Arts and Sciences

Being a minority, as well as being Muslim, affects the way I go about my day at UVA. Certain spaces I won't go to because I don't feel comfortable in it. There are certain classes I won't take. There are certain classes I will take because I can be in that atmosphere where we're talking about those issues, especially if I know there's going to be more minority students in that class, I would think it's a good idea to take that class. I know my first year coming into UVA, I really wanted to have connections with other Black people on campus. One of the classes I chose was "Race, Racism, Colony, and Nation." I knew that would be a class that would attract other minority students, which was true. My professor was Black, which was a really nice experience. I know a lot of people, they'll go through all four years without having a Black professor or even a minority professor, which is bad when you're just getting initiated into the University.

For me, I was lucky. I think three out of four of my professors last year were people of color. I think in any class, especially if you are in a class that's majority white students, you're going to want to have at least the professor, or a TA be a minority. Seeing that makes me feel more comfortable. It makes me feel like I can approach this professor, that this professor is going to be more understanding of my concerns, more understanding of what's going on in my life. It's that similar bond of being at a principally white institution and just being a minority. Not only in the University, but in America. One of the big ones, for me recently, has been having an advisor who is a person of color. She's African American. That's made a big impact on me. She's kind of my personal cheerleader; she always cheers me on. I know I'm really lucky because some students, their advisors do not care at all. They can see that. I think two weeks back I was really frustrated. I was having a hard time managing my time, and I went to talk to her. She's trying to help me manage my time and everything. She was like, "You know what, you need to treat yourself." She goes in her wallet; she takes out $10. She said, "Go find somewhere nice to eat, do your homework, and just relax," which was really nice because it was just that small act of kindness that really made my day.

"I WAS HURT. I FELT LIKE MY VOICE WASN'T BEING HEARD ABOUT HOW OFFENSIVE THAT ACT WAS TO ME."

R.M.

R.M.'s narrative initiates a conversation that details the experience of not being fully supported by the UVA administration. In doing so, R.M. discusses a traumatic experience experienced on-Grounds and hurt caused by feeling unsupported by their dean. R.M's experience is then further articulated by Muslim students at UVA, who discuss the lack of response to anti-Muslim incidents both on and off-Grounds.

I personally find that a lot of my peers are not very knowledgeable about Islam, particularly within the Commerce School. The Comm School attracts a certain type of student: students who are Caucasian, from wealthier backgrounds, who tend to be more right-leaning, more Republican. I had this experience as one of the few Muslim girls in the school. We were working in groups in my third year because students are assigned to a block, which is an assigned classroom that you have for the entire year. It's very different because instead of a 400-person lecture, you're in a 30-person class. You get to know your classmates really really well. But because you get to know them really well, you also get to know their thoughts and opinions as well.

So I could tell they were not very aware of anything that was different from them. Since they were white and wealthy, they would just sometimes state racial stereotypes casually and think that it was okay to do so. There was mimicking of a Black lady saying really rude things. I called one of my peers in the Comm School out. Then there was one of our Chinese students. She was with another older man who is also Chinese. She'd just received a scholarship. We were notified in our block, "Oh, congratulations to your peer." One of my classmates made the assumption "Oh, is that her dad?" This was really insensitive. Just because she was with another older Asian man, they just assumed it was her dad.

Although nothing was directly said negatively about Islam, I always felt different from everyone else. I felt like my voice wasn't as important as their voices at that time. I definitely felt like I was more of a visible symbol of the religion. I also used to wear a hijab. When I did wear the headscarf, people just automatically assumed things about me. Obviously, you're very visibly Muslim when you wear a scarf so people will assume that you're very religious or that you're very extreme in your views. If there's someone who maybe doesn't agree with what they think Muslims believe, I realized, they won't say anything straight to your face. I've never had anything said straight to my face. Not many people would ask me directly about my beliefs. It wasn't really brought up much. But I still felt the implicit bias.

I'd be sitting on a bus and, literally, all the seats were taken. There'd be one seat next to me. The bus would be cramped, right? No one would sit at that seat. I remember not feeling as safe walking back home from the library late at night, especially during the time of the election and after Trump was elected. I was a first-year student, just me by myself, and I was really afraid for my safety. My peers and my friends were also afraid for me to walk late from the library as a hijabi because I'd be a visible target for someone, especially when all that fear mongering was going on.

I also have Muslim friends who were the target of such offenses. They were both hijabis. One of them was followed in a car. They were three white guys. They basically followed her as she was walking. It was later at night. They were yelling names and things at her. I also had another friend who lived in Brown College, and someone wrote the word "terrorist" outside of her door. There are just many weird microaggressions that I would *feel*.

Talking about all of these moments just reminded me of something. Do you know when something bad happens to you, you kind of tend to block it out? I did have something happen to me at UVA that was really hard. It was my second year, towards the end of the year. I was walking in Nau Gibson. I was minding my own business. It was towards the end of the Spring semester; stuff was wrapping up. I was having a really hard time that semester. I was super stressed out. I was walking and talking on my phone. I'm walking, there's a group of three white girls that are walking this way and I'm walking that way. I'm not thinking anything of it, minding my own business. One of them goes, "Terrorist." She was with her friends. They all started laughing. I didn't think I heard properly, so I was like, "What?" So I just kept walking. Then she turned around. They started walking towards me. They were walking opposite to where I was walking. When I kept walking that way, she turned around and yelled it louder. And I definitely knew I heard it the second time. She was like, "Terrorist!" This was when I was wearing the hijab, so you definitely know that I'm Muslim.

I got scared because the fact that she had stopped in her path with her friends who were all just giggling, then she had turned around to say it towards me, and I thought they were going to start following me. The hallway was pretty isolated. So, I walked really really fast to get more towards where other people were, and then I just cried. That was the tipping point of a really stressful time for me. I didn't understand why me, minding my own business, not doing anything, would make someone say something really hurtful. It was harder because it was multiple people against one. The thing was that there were a lot of professors' offices in that area. I don't know how it could be that no one heard because she was pretty loud about it. It was very aggressive, not even in a giggly way. It was meant to be heard. It was meant to be harsh. I literally ran and hid near the Starbucks, where there's a little cave area because I didn't know, I couldn't tell whether she was following me. I just walked really fast and tried to get towards people.

Afterwards, I went to speak to my dean about it. I reported it through UVA's *Your Right to Know* because you can report hate crimes on that as well. Then I was called in by my dean. I asked if they could try to go back and look in the video recording systems to see who they were and identify them. That never resulted in anything. No one ended up getting in trouble for it. I don't think that's an issue in itself. I don't think that the dean responded as well as she could have to the situation. When I think about it, if it was any other religious group that had been called a slur like that, whether it was an African American, whether it was a Jewish student, if they had been called something offensive, I feel like the university would have cared more.

I was hurt. I felt like my voice wasn't being heard about how offensive that act was to me. I was so scared. No one should feel unsafe, especially within a university building during the daylight hours, nor should they be called that slur. Sometimes I think that the university chooses what to release to students. There are biases in that. I think if the same thing was said to a Jewish student, something anti-Semitic, it would have blown up. But, unfortunately, as a Muslim, if someone calls me a terrorist, they're just like, "Okay, do you want us to talk to your professors and give you extensions on your assignment?" That's literally what my dean said. She was like, "Okay, I understand this is a hard time. I can reach out to your professors. We can get your deadlines pushed back." Not like, "Oh, what can we do to make this university safer and inclusive?" What makes it sad was that that dean was an African American woman. And I think if it was another African American person who went to her and said, "This is what happened to me. Someone called me something terrible, the N-word" or something, that would have blown up. But for me, coming as a Muslim, and saying, "Someone called me a terrorist," she was like, "Okay, well, how can we support you?" The school didn't respond well at all. They were really dismissive about it.

And then the third year, one day when I was walking home from school in the early evening. I lived on Jefferson Park Avenue (JPA). As I was walking past some white guy, he whispered "KKK" under his breath. It was scary because I was all alone and JPA can get pretty isolated. I was wearing my scarf at the time as well. There was literally no one else on the street at that time, or at least not visibly near. I was so scared, I ran all the way because it was a terrible feeling to have someone saying something that to me, something as radical as the "KKK," and what that implies when you say that to a person of color.' It's really harsh.

Fadumo Hussein
Class of 2023
College of Arts and Sciences

In my "Writing and Rhetoric" class, we were looking at a cover of a book called *Citizen* by Claudia Rankine. It was a picture of a hoodie. It was just the top part of the hoodie on this white backdrop. However, when we were going over the analysis of a book cover, this girl made the comment that maybe the hoodie was trying to cover something and referenced *The Handmaid's Tale*. She saw that covering as a sign of oppression. Being a Muslim who wears a hijab, I was really taken aback. Black students were trying to point to how the hoodie can be used as a way to express being hyper-visible and invisible at the same time, but this student saw that as oppression. She cited *The Handmaid's Tale* first, which is an explicit example, but then she went broader to say coverings are oppressive. I was like "Ugh."

Still, although I've been here for only approximately 11 to 12 weeks, I haven't seen anything explicitly that necessarily would make me fearful. No one has really explicitly said anything negative or done anything where I was treated as a stereotype. I came from a very white school. To give you a reference, I was the only graduating hijabi in my entire class. So, there was always this sense of hyper-visibility. If there was ever a global issue, let's say a terrorist organization, an attack happening, people would always say, "What's your input on this? Why do you participate in this?" I came into UVA, then, with a background of always trying to have to explain myself. I didn't necessarily come in with a guard, but I always felt like, in a sense, I had to do the labor that could be done by the person asking the question. You just need to take time to look up information. It became very tiring over time. I came into UVA with that expectation that I would be tired from trying to simultaneously deal with that issue and with school. I was excited for the new environment, but I always kept in the back of my head that, "Oh you might have to do this." I was trying to think of ways I could go about changing it and not tire myself out by having to constantly explain my existence. So far, I've had to explain mostly things just out of curiosity by a friend or classmate, which I'm not opposed to doing. It was just someone asking the meaning of the hijab and other religious questions. It was more of a sense of them being curious and trying to understand rather than, "Oh you have to explain that what you're doing is not wrong in this context when across the world it's wrong."

Javaria Abbasi
Class of 2020
College of Arts and Sciences

A few years ago, there was the *Tree of Life* shooting in Pittsburgh. UVA issued an official condemnation. But when Muslims were attacked in the New Zealand Mosque shooting, there was no official condemnation by UVA. I think a lot of Muslim students were really impacted by that psychologically. There was this horrible cognitive dissonance going to class and seeing the no one knew how much it impacted you. It just seemed like people didn't care. I don't think the support we get from administration is all that fair.

K.S.

For Muslims, UVA administration could be so much better. I had a huge problem my first year with UVA's former president, Teresa Sullivan. It was the night of September 11th, so the anniversary of 9/11. Someone had put a bunch of posters up on the dorms with fake statistics about Black people, Jewish people, and Muslim people. Housing and Residence Life took the posters down in the morning before most people saw them. It was concentrated towards first year dorms, so that's why it was more relevant to me. I remember Sullivan's email right after that happened. It was like a few lines long. It didn't say anything about what she was going to do to prevent this from happening again. She sent maybe one measly paragraph about the posters that were put up around first-year dorms. I know people who have faced similar microaggressions. The administration response to these incidents was also very disappointing. But later when someone did something to the Jefferson statue, she sent four long paragraphs about why that was wrong. I remember reading that statement. I was just disgusted. Why would you think more about a statue than a person?

I just wished that those subtle, soft, yet impactful acts of hatred were recognized. I think that there needs to be an actual punishment. There needs to be an actual investigation done. I just wish that they would do something. I think that when Sullivan was president, the "investigations" that were being done weren't sincere at all. I didn't feel like I was being protected. No one ever found out who did the posters thing. I *know* there's surveillance at UVA. They definitely have surveillance at UVA. I don't know why they wouldn't know. I think Jim Ryan is probably going to try to tackle that in a couple of years, but I can't help but feel like people like me will always be on the back burner. I'm okay as long as administration can be sincere about their goals to try to make sure that students feel safe here by actually pursuing people who do such acts. It's just difficult to feel comforted and safe by their actions because most of what I've experienced is prolonged inaction. In my mind, that sincerity is wrapped in layers of doubt.

I just wish that I knew that if something happened to me, they would be able to know who did it. I wish that UVA would be able to support me. I think that UVA students on the whole are pretty nice about it. They're pretty curious, they want to know. They're not going to pretend that they know everything about the religion based on what they've heard. I think students have been very vocal about this kind of thing. They recognize that these are things that happen here at the university. I don't think the students have really much to do with the administration deciding to do an investigation or not. If they feel strongly enough about it, they'll speak out. Overall, I think the students are pretty well-off in terms of fostering a community that feels welcoming to me.

"IT'S GETTING MORE DIFFICULT TO PUBLICLY IDENTIFY ONESELF AS A MUSLIM"

T.J.

T.J.'s narrative initiates a consideration of being "physically seen as a Muslim student" and the consequent sense of feeling threatened and "targeted" as a result. In the process, T.J. recounts the many instances of how recent events in Charlottesville have led to "the Grounds" feeling unsafe for many Muslim students. These same students then build upon T.J's experiences to discuss similar moments of being "visible" within and beyond classrooms by, for example, wearing a hijab. As such, these students help us to understand how the public perception of one's identity can directly impact their experiences in academic and social settings.

Earlier in 2017, when white nationalists, the KKK, and Richard Spencer came to Charlottesville, I found that really frightening. That was two weeks before I started my freshman year of college. My mom was literally saying, "I think it's time to transfer to VCU." The events were a genuine safety concern. My mom still exhibits those concerns. We talk every day, but if I'm ever out late at night, she's so concerned. She remembers those events. She says, "I'm just so scared that something might happen to you. You never know what kind of hate crime you'd run into." And it's devastating! It's devastating to see your parents fear so much for your safety. The white nationalists, they target foreigners, Muslim people, or anyone who is not like them. So me being in the "Other" category in their eyes, that puts me at an immediate risk. That additional risk is one of the reasons that makes me scared to walk out at three in the morning. Somebody might do something to me not just because I'm a woman or a person that they could've attacked, but also because I'm a Muslim. The color of my skin is different. I'm brown, so that is indicative that I could likely be of a different ethnicity. That difference in skin color is a quick identifier. It may cause them to take action. You never know what somebody's motive might be. You never know what somebody's immediate thoughts or prejudices deep down are and what they think of you.

These concerns emerged after the Charlottesville incident where people realized that such kinds of racist outbursts and actions could actually happen at UVA. Before that, it was simply thought that it could happen anywhere, but then it actually happened in Charlottesville. Now when people talk about Charlottesville, they think about that event. People's perception of Charlottesville has changed. Because the events of August 11th had happened, the possibility that such incidents could actually take place here are confirmed in people's minds.[1] Therefore, it is hard to not think about it and be fearful. Therefore, a fear of mine is of being attacked.

My mother continues to have this concern, this fear, since day one, since the incident in Charlottesville, and even before then. In fact, it is one of the reasons why I don't even wear a hijab; I just don't want to give even more identifiers. Even though I'm religious and I value Islam so much, I don't want to put myself in a position where somebody can be further prejudiced against me. I always have these thoughts deep down, so it's not just about UVA. For instance, there was an incident in Richmond where a man called a bunch of Muslim girls in a gymnasium who were just there for an event "terrorists." He was expressing blatant Islamophobia. I've thought to myself, "If he can hold these prejudices, anybody can!" That event happened around VCU, another university, so I don't think that it's outside of the reach that this university can have people who have the same belief systems. It might not be something that you actively think about every day, but it is a constant concern that is always present in the back of your mind.

If somebody asked me a direct question, "Oh, are you Muslim?" I have no problem answering, "Yeah, absolutely!" I'm proud of being Muslim. However, it varies depending on the situation. For example, I had this interaction the other day. There are often a lot of Christian groups on-Grounds that come out. They'll want to inform people about Christianity. They'll come out, obviously, with the intention to inform and possibly convert people. They hand out Bibles and everything. I've been stopped quite a few times. Even though I am a Muslim, I'm not uncomfortable talking to them because I like having the conversation. I know that there are differences. I like learning about the differences. However, the other day, one of the Christian leaders who came with those groups, after finding out that I was a Muslim, asked me "Why don't you wear a headscarf?" He asked, quite aggressively, "If you're scared of going to hell then why don't you wear a headscarf?" It made me uncomfortable. It made me wary to tell certain older white adults that I'm

---

1   The events of August 11th and 12th refers to the Unite the Right rally which was a white supremacist rally that took place in Charlottesville, Virginia in 2017. (New York Times, 2017)

Muslim when I don't have to do so. When they asked questions like that, I couldn't tell them it's because I'm scared of people like you.'

I don't want to categorize a group, nor a demographic as a whole, but what I've seen with some figures makes me cautious. If I were to be on a bus, for example, and there's some people who I perceive would not really be tolerant or comfortable with a Muslim being there, then I won't point out my religion. I won't make it known. I think that threatens my own safety, and they also feel threatened by me, based on stereotypes. So I have definitely been in these kinds of situations where I've held back from telling people that I'm Muslim at UVA and outside of UVA because I am scared. I'm scared of people on the bus, or in public, giving me dirty looks because I'm wearing a hijab. I'm scared of people pulling it off or even targeting me because of it.

There are so many instances of hate crimes towards women for wearing hijabs. In fact, there was one the other day. A woman was really beaten and stomped on the head, just due to blatant Islamophobia. Furthermore, I notice the looks that people give my mom when she wears a hijab on Eid Day in public. I notice the comments that other people make towards my other Muslim friends when they say they're from a Muslim country, like "Oh, are you a terrorist?" When I was younger, someone learned my last name and told me, "That sounds like a terrorist name." This was in sixth grade, so a group of kids just called me a terrorist for the rest of the year. My dad's name is Mohammed. I couldn't even imagine the amount of fear that he must have had after the 9/11 events. He has never really spoken on it except just saying that he was fearful. I could sense it. He was extremely fearful that something would happen to him, that his wife and his daughter, who didn't have really outstanding or identifiable Muslim names, would need to go on or grow up without him. It is these kinds of things that make me so fearful of wearing a hijab or displaying my identity as a Muslim. It makes you have to shut yourself down. It makes you have to be fearful because you're concerned for your safety, or Mom's safety, or Dad's safety.

I told my parents many years ago I was going to put on a hijab once I got to university. Then the Charlottesville rally happened. Then the accumulation of all of the things that I saw, like the hate crime reports and the hate crimes that increased in the past couple of years due to the national administration's careless comments. Voices become louder of the people who act on all these prejudices. Nobody's stopping them, and, as a result, there is a huge anti-Muslim sentiment. It's just getting more and more difficult to be able to fully identify oneself as a Muslim without feeling like you're going to be harmed or be made an outcast.

M.B.

I wasn't a hijabi my first year. I actually put on the hijab the summer after my first year, because I was visiting overseas, and I thought it was finally time for me. So I have had that perspective of passing as white with my hair out. I also have the perspective of being an outward sign of Islam on-Grounds. I think that definitely contributes a lot to my perception of being Muslim because I've seen it from both sides– as somebody who wasn't easily identifiable as Muslim and as someone who is easily identifiable. I actually went to a Muslim private school in Northern Virginia from second grade to seventh grade. So I have quite a lot of understanding from my classes about Islam, particularly how it applies to our lifestyle as second-generation Muslims in America. That definitely contributes to my overall perception.

Before I became a hijabi, I think that my first impressions of a lot of people were mostly focused on my achievements, my goals in life, my career goals as a woman. Not a lot of that was tied to my ethnicity or my religion because at the time, nothing about me outwardly indicated that I wasn't "American." I didn't necessarily volunteer about my religion unless asked. I wasn't ashamed of it or anything. For me, it's just part of my identity. I didn't necessarily feel the need to push it into every conversation. "Oh, by the way, I'm Muslim and I'm Palestinian," you know?

Before the hijab, all of my first impressions mostly dealt with my personality and my academic career here. After I became a visible Muslim when I was wearing the hijab, my first impression quickly became that I "most likely wasn't born here." So a lot of the conversations shifted into "Where are you from?" not, "What are you trying to do? What are you studying?" It's "Where are you from?", "What languages do you speak?" "Welcome to our country. What country do you come from?" and "You're clearly Muslim. You're clearly multicultural. That's awesome." The topic quickly changed from my personal career goals to the topic of diversity and inclusion. It became about my experience here as a Muslim woman, not so much a woman that was "pre-Comm."

I put on my hijab last year so I have that dual experience of having some of my friends not even recognize me. They walked right past me because all they saw was the scarf. I thought that was pretty interesting. I think that my perspective of how people treated me differently, I think that's one of the biggest reasons I chose to do this interview is because I can talk about how I'm treated differently as a hijabi. I don't know if that's a good or bad thing.

Javaria Abbasi
Class of 2020
College of Arts and Sciences

I think that what people first notice about me is my height and then my hijab. I am so tall, even if I'm just making passing comments on-Grounds, I always feel noticed. I can't really play off my Muslimness, and I don't want to. I definitely think that it means I have to be much more willing to engage with people who just are visiting Grounds or just want to have a discussion about Islam. I will just get stopped randomly. And as a first year, I found this more discomforting because I didn't know UVA culture that well. I hadn't done debate here specifically. But as a fourth year, it doesn't really bother me. In fact, I sometimes like it because I would rather correct people's misconceptions directly than have them continue believing certain things. Obviously, I think the discomfiture or the spectacular nature of being a hijabi at UVA is particular to UVA because there are fewer Muslims in proportion to the rest of the population.

Whereas my sister goes to George Mason University which has a huge Muslim population. People don't really bat an eye when we walk around. I've never felt even looked at the way that I do sometimes at UVA. I've definitely never been stalked or asked questions about Islam or being Islamic. UVA is a bit different. I'm in a sorority and I think that that can definitely be a problem for some. I have found fraternity men make a lot of assumptions based on my appearance on what I like or don't like. They just make comments about whether I should or should not be in sorority based on my religious beliefs. They ask if I'm actually following my religion. It's very interesting that people feel more entitled in social settings to do that than intellectual settings.

My professors are very respectful of my religion. Many of them see it as an asset rather than something that takes away from my interpretations of class content. Specifically, since I have studied religion and theology historically, I can speak beyond generalizations which my professors find helpful because, often, they cannot do so. I'm willing to correct them. Most of them appreciate it. I haven't really had a problem directly with a professor in that regard. I think that for professors who don't know me, there's this weird assumption that Muslim women don't speak up in class, don't know how to put their ideas forward, especially as hijabis. They think hijabis will be very quiet. But I have almost nine years of debate experience, so I'm definitely not that. I think it was almost funny the first time I raised my hand in class to see how professors react because some of them are a little bit more shocked and some of them are not. That small moment can, in my mind, let me gauge a lot about that person.

K.S.

I think because I started wearing it recently, the hijab was the first thing students noticed about me. It's like the hijab, then my race, and then it's just other things. I think the hijab is the first thing noticed because it's the most obvious thing, but I don't think that students really think anything of it because there are Muslims here on-Grounds. On the whole, they understand that you can't really judge a person based on one thing that person wears. But I do feel not necessarily singled out but that I can't mess up. I now represent Islam to people who maybe have never even heard about Islam. I feel a certain pressure to perform, to be good, to not fall asleep in lecture, or whatever. At the same time, I don't think that people presume anything about me from the get-go. They generally want to be kind to people.

When I leave Grounds, I don't really think about the hijab because I'm not in that close classroom space. I'm out in the open. You can't really think anything about a person's background if you're out in the open. It doesn't really matter as much because my peers, my professors, they all affect how I'm doing. They all affect my environment and that's really important to me. But when I'm off-Grounds, I can just go somewhere else and change my environment. I don't really think about it when I'm out there. When I'm here at UVA, I think about it.

Wearing the hijab is very encouraging rather than burdening. I think it's more of an encouragement for me to do better. I have more incentive to do better for others than I do just for myself. If I'm representing Muslims to other people, I feel like that's more important for me to care about how I act. That is why I do have pressure to perform. There's an incentive to perform, but I wouldn't necessarily call it a burden because I like it. It pushes me to be a better person, and I'm thankful for it.

Sara Ali
Class of 2021
College of Arts and Sciences
Class of 2022
McIntire School of Commerce

I think many people at UVA see me positively. They see me as someone who worked hard to get here. I think they put a story to me sometimes. They'll assume I'm a harder worker. They'll assume, "Oh, this Muslim girl, she's a really good student." They'll just assume positive things about me. I don't complain. You could tell from the interaction that they assume I'm such a good girl. I'm not saying I'm not a good girl, but I'm not the best, either. So it's interesting getting that treatment here at UVA. I do love it. I really do. Even outside of UVA, when I travel with friends, I still sometimes receive better treatment from other people because of my hijab. They respect me. I know this is completely opposite of what people expect, but it's my personal experience.

P.E.

In my Engagement class, "What is Engaged Citizenship," we talked about student culture at UVA. I have this friend who's on the First Year Council. She's a hijabi. She was talking about how she wears her religion outside publicly, how people receive it, how she's scared because it's not typical to see a hijabi on UVA Grounds. We discussed that in class. She feels really vulnerable wearing it because she's telling everyone that she's Muslim by wearing it. That makes her a target sometimes. In that way, I felt my teacher in that class gave her a platform to talk about it in a safe space. I liked getting to hear that from another Muslim in a class where I didn't think I would see any other people like me. I felt good in that class, and my teacher was really nice about it.

Faris Musa
Class of 2020
McIntire School of Commerce

I want to give my experience, which I would assume is probably radically different than a minority Muslim, a Brown/Black Muslim, whatever label you want to throw there. It's very different because I am a white Muslim. I don't shy away from that issue because my skin color is my skin color. This is how Allah created me. I can't change anything about it. Of course, there's definitely going to be a difference in how people treat me than how people treat Brown/Black Muslims, but I believe that it's still important to get my perspective. We'd love to think that we can be neutral and objective, but I'm sure I do have my own biases, my own subjective nature to everything that I've just said. Things I said may have been inaccurate. They could have been accurate. It's dependent on a ton of many variables.

The difference in treatment between me and, say, a Brown or Black or another type of Muslim that's a minority or considered a minority, has both racial and religious roots. It might be more racial, but there's definitely an intersection. Let's take gender bias, racial bias, and then religious bias. Let's take an African American Muslim female wearing a hijab, that's like three strikes. First, she's a woman; second, she's Black; and third, she has a hijab on. Women already face their own struggles as it is. Then, women of color face their own individual struggles. And now, you're adding Islam to that mix as well. It's struggles on top of struggles on top of struggles. The way people treat her is going to be so much more different than how people are going to treat a white invisibly Muslim man. I am invisibly Muslim; people can't tell that I'm Muslim. I'm a white male who is invisibly Muslim. People are going to treat me like I'm a white male without the religious component. That is how society is!

A lot of people try to overcompensate when they see someone who is an African American female, for example. They try to overcompensate in being nice, but they don't realize that that in itself is a bias in its own way because there's still a differential component there. You're still treating them differently. I mean, I've seen it on teams. I'm probably guilty of it myself - I can't lie. It'd be impossible for anyone to tell me that they weren't guilty of it. Everyone has prejudices against everyone, and while it is impossible to completely eliminate, it is possible to mitigate.

If people could tell that I am a Muslim at face value, I really don't know if their treatment of me, or interaction with me, would have been different. I would assume *yes* because my sister is a hijabi third-year student who is also white. She's also in the Comm School. I can blatantly see her treatment being different. I don't know if it would be worse treatment or if it would just be them reacting to their natural biases, which again, in my opinion, you can't inhibit your biases 100%. It's actually a part of us. A ton of other psychological studies and other research that has been conducted has said that you physically cannot stop your unconscious bias. Therefore, we can do our best to mitigate them, but we can't get rid of them completely. So the treatment definitely would be different because those biases might come into play.

K.G.

UVA students don't notice that I'm an Arab Muslim at first. That comes later. That's the second thing they notice. Even within the Arab population, you have an issue of white privilege. Since I very much look white, I think in my classes, in the social setting that I'm in, in my extracurriculars people's first assumption is that I'm white. That's what their first interpretation of me is, and it softens or opens up their willingness to get to know me. At that point, when I reveal that I'm actually an Arab Muslim, I'm Palestinian-Syrian, it becomes a point of interest and intrigue. "Oh wow, I would have never taken you for that." This is different than for someone who wears a hijab or someone who's visibly "Other." I think that's the first thing people notice about them. Then people, whether or not they want to, whether or not it's conscious, will draw unfair conclusions.

I think this is a problem, but it's a problem that I've benefited from personally. They don't immediately look at me as an "Other," so when I tell them my name, when I tell them where I'm from, there's no inherent tension because at that point whatever misconception they might have or whatever Otherness they've assigned to someone else, that doesn't exist. It becomes a teachable opportunity for me where they might ask me where my name is from. That opens the door for me to begin to educate and begin to inform. This is a giant privilege, but I don't think I've ever experienced a sharp change in treatment from what someone had thought I was to what I actually am after they find out. It just seems more like they're intrigued and want to learn more at that point. Instead of having to overcome that barrier from the beginning, it kind of eases them into it, if that makes sense.

"I THINK CERTAIN SECTIONS
ARE DEFINITELY IMPROVING"

K.G.

K.G.'s narrative initiates a consideration of being Muslim within the culture of UVA which seems increasingly committed to improving the situation of marginalized student communities. K.G. notes that from the outside, UVA may seem to be a privileged space. They highlight, however, that there is an active shift by student groups to acknowledge and address sense of privilege as well as the consequences for those communities which such privilege excludes. Drawing from their own experiences, Muslim students at UVA detail how as part of these efforts many UVA student organizations are trying (or are not trying) to understand Islam and its practices.

UVA is a very privileged and white space to begin with. You have to be very conscious of that wherever you go, the courses that you take, the professors that you're learning from, knowing that the space that you're in is a privileged and white one. I think that is something that anyone who's not white is always conscious of, whether they're in the classroom, in their extracurriculars, or in their involvements. It's just something that you're aware of. But with that said, I think the greatest thing about this university is the academics, first and foremost, because there are so many resources in terms of the professors that you have, in terms of the content and access to material that you have here, that even though you're in a privileged and white space, you have resources that you can use to explore that, and working with professors to explore where you fit.

One of the things that I've noticed over the course of my four years here is that the school is divided in a lot of ways. There's Greek life, there's Student Council, there are minorities who kind of also have their own spaces or form their own space. Whether it's physical or not is a separate thing. But, I think, despite all of that, I see a very clear eagerness from a lot of students to learn how to acknowledge that privilege and acknowledge white privilege in specific, as it relates to this university as well as the very deep and entrenched racist problematic (in many ways) history that UVA embodies. I think we do have a student body that's very curious and is actively taking strides towards moving forward from it and moving forward in a way that's constructive and a way that hasn't necessarily been done before.

The conversations from my first year to my fourth year that I've heard have gone miles beyond what I would've expected. I think the atmosphere around Grounds is a white space, but the student body as a whole is really showing clear signs of taking steps to address that issue and to find a real solution to making this space intersectional, to making it welcoming to minority students, to low-income students, to first gen students. They are committed to creating an atmosphere where that long entrenched history can now be addressed in some way and be confronted. I think that's become pretty evident over the last couple of years here.

I think certain sections are definitely improving. I don't think the Comm School kids, maybe the Engineering School kids, are exposed as often to the material that would confront that or address that history, are learning about how and why the university became such a privileged white space. They're not going to have an opportunity to take those classes or work with those professors who have such a depth of knowledge about the topic. I do think it is a certain section of the school, but it's a section of the school that has the widest reach. While it's not the whole student body, those students are the ones that are involved in a lot of different corners of the university. The perspectives that they're learning, the academics that they're studying, the passions that they're pursuing will end up being felt by different sections of the University because they're the ones that are spread out the most. But with that said, I don't think it's a university-wide thing. I think we're far from where it's a university-wide thing. I just mean in the sense that it's very clear that there's an active movement towards that.

After August 11th and 12ᵗʰ 2017, the Black Student Alliance made the demand for a required curriculum that would address the history of slavery at the university, but that seems a very bureaucratic process. There's just a lot of red tape around how you can get that to happen. On the one hand it's a great idea to have a curriculum where students are exposed to that history. But on the flip side, if the Engineering School kids or Comm School kids take one class, I don't think that's anywhere near enough to address something as deep as Islamophobia, Anti-Semitism, racism, all of that. Just taking a single class your first year when you just came to the university, that's not going to solve the problem on its own. One of the ways that I think would be just a more active effort from the administration is to acknowledge the issues in an equitable way - not shining light on a particular issue more than another issue. The more the administration can be in conversations and receptive to the Muslim community, the Jewish community, the Black community, the

Latinx community, the more involved and aware they are of what's going on in those communities, the more that the administration can respond. That can be in a variety of ways, such as in hiring a diverse set of faculty members and making sure that there's a wider variety of courses taught that are open for students to take them. I think that's how it translates.

The administration needs to become aware, and, by becoming aware, can set in motion more institutional decisions that can address Islamophobia in its entirety and its complexity. It's really hard to envision a set specific way: "This is the problem, here's the solution." If it was as easy as that, I think we would've seen a very clear blueprint, and we don't have one. That's kind of why it's up to a lot of the students here to guide that conversation because they know what they need, they know their surroundings, and they know where to take it.

Y.H.

UVA is open to Islam but is very ignorant towards the actual practice and knowledge that, in general, people should possess. I've seen and gone through a lot of Minority Rights Coalition, UJC, and other CIOs as well as a lot of other different aspects of UVA, even including frats because I've done work with them, too. The biggest thing I've noticed is that a lot of minority students, POCs, even religious minorities, they all know about Islam. They know we don't eat pork, we don't do this, and we don't do that, and whatnot. But everyone else, they don't seem to know at all. Even at UVA, I have people saying, "Oh, are you an Islam?" We're like, "You know, that's not what you say? You say 'Muslim.' Islam is the overarching religion." So the atmosphere of UVA, while its campus is very safe as regards Islamic issues, I'd say it's very ignorant. We didn't break that bubble of getting the general population to understand us yet.

They don't teach people much about Islam in public schools. They just teach "the five pillars." That's basically it. Even here, people ask me, "What do you guys believe in?" It's the same thing. We believe in Heaven, Hell. God is one God. But people really are very ignorant towards the actual specifics. Not even specifics, just in general; they are ignorant about what we do practice, like praying five times a day, that we don't eat this, and we don't drink that.

People really don't care to seek out the information. A lot of people will just get into their studies and won't go outside of that framework. They just stay up in their room. People are a part of a club so they don't get out much, like frats, for example. Frats don't do many initiatives to get more diversity in their culture. I've seen frats talk to the Muslim Student Association, but, yeah, a lot of the bigger umbrella doesn't get to us. So do people understand Islam, the broader sense of, like, the majority of the community here? No, I'd say no for sure.

M. Ahmad

One thing that UVA should improve upon is having more of an understanding of the religion of Islam. I think that would go a long way. I think educating about, or being more supportive of, Islam is important for creating hospitality and learning from each other. If our professors aren't aware of what Islam actually is, historically or religiously, if they're just following the news or just following their own biases or generalizations that they've heard, that can be harmful for the atmosphere at UVA and for making progress as a community. I think it starts with the professors as they are the ones who dictate the atmosphere of their classrooms. From an academic standpoint, they are the ones in power in the classrooms and who can bring forth discussions that can challenge student viewpoints. Not only do such discussions help decrease stereotypes that students might hold, they create a better understanding of our Muslim community within the UVA community. At the end of the day, professors shouldn't be misrepresenting Islam since it can be harmful to students. It only spreads falsehood and possibly hate. From my personal experience in classes where the professors were knowledgeable about Islam, the class was a refreshing experience for the Muslims and an informative one for those who do not know much about Islam. I definitely think having students know more about Islam is really helpful, too. If someone grows up only hearing one side of the story, they may be less likely to be open to change later on in their lives.

I have seen the support that Dean Groves and former President Teresa Sullivan gave our community when incidents happened on-Grounds or in the local community against Muslims. I am glad that the administration is reaching out and showing their support. Of course, every administration response cannot be expected to be perfect and there is room for improvement, but the moments of support we received were appreciated. Since we have programs, such as diversity training, that show support for different groups, genders, orientations, and races, I believe some sort of optional religious training may also be beneficial. Having a discussion on major religions would be good, too. It could go a long way to help bring more understanding about Islam.

CHAPTER TWO
Culture

C.P., M.B., Mazzen Shalaby, Rawan Osman, K.G., Sara Ali, I.F., Ilyas Saltani, Shahira Ali, Ahmed Hussain, Fadumo Hussein, Khadeja Muhammed, P.E., Javaria Abbasi, K.S., Y.H., Al Ahmed, Hisham Ahmad

Culture seems a static term, set. It is also an indication of possible growth. In this chapter, students speak to the difficult work of animating the possibilities inherent in the UVA student culture. They speak from a recognition that "student culture," as a set of attitudes and practices, seems stuck. It is unable to allow the possibilities of new identities and voices to inform its classrooms, organizations, and offices. As a result, Muslim students often fail to get the public support required to ensure their education at UVA is not marked by bigotry, verbal attacks, and violence. The administration, they argue, has historically been unwilling to speak out against attacks against Muslims on-Grounds or in the larger community. Muslim students, these students, are often forced to rely on the individual efforts of particular faculty or administrators. It's a solution to the immediate incident but an inadequate strategy to reform the general culture. And throughout this chapter, these students provide glimpses of what a student and university culture might look like if the full manifestation of cultures, heritages, and traditions were nurtured, supported. These voices demonstrate that a limited static culture damages the potential of certain populations directly but, in doing so, limits the possibilities and promise of entire UVA student culture. Ultimately, these students speak to the possibility (and need) for growth.

"THE CLIMATE HERE IS EXHAUSTING
TO STUDENTS OF COLOR"

C.P.

C.P.'s narrative initiates a consideration of the importance of allyship and safe spaces within the university, spaces where minority students can engage in meaningful ways to understand their experiences at UVA. To highlight this need, C.P. discusses instances where they had to deal with students' inappropriate actions towards them and feeling unfairly challenged in their classes. Building off these examples, Muslim students at UVA expand the discussion to express frustration at the general lack of knowledge about Islam in the larger student community.

I am a Political & Social Thought major, but I study African American Studies as well. Those classes are always very easy because I'm learning, I'm absorbing, and I don't have to do any emotional labor to bring in my minority perspective. A lot of times in the Politics department, however, we study theory without really considering the people that it applies to in real life. That affects me, having come originally from Egypt – a country with a very clear post-colonial legacy. British colonization left a heavy impact on the country, socially and economically. That strain continues to this day. Being Muslim, being North African, being Middle Eastern comes with a political identity that you can't really make go away. It translates into my own thoughts, opinions, and analysis on any academic work that I do.

It can be really frustrating being in the Politics department, hearing professors admire and talk about different theorists whose ideas clearly only apply to Western nations, and that, otherwise, would be quite imperialist. One of the theorists that I would think of is Aga Khan, who's studied pretty often. He offers these general definitions of democracy. These definitions are very uncomfortable to me because I know how much they've defined American foreign policy. In the Middle East, we have a joke. It goes, "Don't piss off America or else they'll bring democracy to your country." It refers to the fact that every time the United States has intervened in a nation, they've done so in the name of *democracy* and the name of *justice*. I think the interventions, though, resulted in just utter devastation of the places. Iraq is, like, a prime example. Libya is another, though a more subvert, intervention. There are other countries as well.

There was one instance that stands out. In one of my classes, we were reading a book, a novel, a fictional novel, called *Hope and Other Dangerous Pursuits*. It follows the story of six or seven Moroccans who are trying to migrate. They are about to get smuggled on a boat across the Mediterranean into Italy or Greece. The situations in their country are so dire that they need to get out, you know? One is being persecuted for being gay, one is being domestically abused by her husband and can't get help, and another is targeted by the government. They have to leave. It was a book that made me very, very emotional. Immigration has been a part of my family's story. I'm still dealing with it right now. I have my citizenship interview in two days. I'm nervous. We had so much trouble just figuring out visas, figuring out documentation, security. It's been such a struggle. We've gone back and forth so often. It has just defined who I am. It has defined my story and my family's story. So, I went into class ready to discuss what I thought was an incredible book only to find the majority of my classmates, most of whom are white because politics classes tend to be white dominated, are very apathetic to the book. They didn't like it. One person said something along the lines of "I didn't really feel compelled to sympathize with the characters in the book." Others were like, "Half the migrants didn't even make it and went back to Morocco and they're living their lives still, so why did they even try to leave in the first place?"

I ended up trying to explain so much of the book to them. All of it was happening, though, in the midst of the period that Deferred Action for Childhood Arrivals (DACA) was rescinded, which I was working on with DREAMers (now *undocUVA*). That was a very emotional process as well. We were working with congressmen and trying to push for different bills in the House in both Richmond and in Washington, D.C. We were rallying to make sure undocumented students in the university were able to continue their education. We're doing all this labor outside of class that's really hard and most of it is a dead end, honestly. I'm dealing with all that emotional work, then suddenly, in class, it's just this group of liberals making such statements.

And that's the thing. None of them are conservative. They're all liberal! They all claim to support these things, and I know they do, theoretically. I don't think any of them are bad people. At that moment in class, though, I just felt detached. It was a moment where I was like, "Oh, there's a wall between me and you. You're not going to put the effort to climb it, so I have to build you a window." It became too much to handle. I don't even remember what one person said, but someone said something that was about the book. I just got so emotional that I ended up having to run out of the classroom because I started crying. I'm not one who casually cries in the middle of a classroom. It's not something that I had ever done before. This particular situation got me to that point. I think that was the peak because there are so many instances like that in most classrooms that are white-dominated— instances of having to constantly explain yourself and your opinions and your analysis, then often being reprimanded for not backing it with theory.

I understand the importance of backing what you say with evidence or theory. But how am I supposed to know the names of theorists who agree with me when no professor ever assigns them to me? Why do I have to do *their* labor of going out on my own to find other readings and books by people from these different parts of the world? Or from these different origins who have these ideas, and who *do* support what I'm saying? There are many such authors. We just don't get assigned to read them in classes, even though they are very relevant. I'm in college to learn, but I'm not learning. There are many classes where I have learned a lot of great stuff, but most of the time I was not getting a diverse education.

I was in a class my second year. It was on American political thought. It was a seminar. It was, like, 20 people, basically 13 white men out of 20. The rest are white women. There were only two students who were people of color: me and one Black man. The professor was obsessed with the founding fathers. On the first day he was like, "Teaching this class, in a pavilion classroom, on Thomas Jefferson's lawn, in his university!" My thought was, "Dude, calm down! That's way too many compliments for a guy who owned 600 slaves and raped them. Chill out." I knew the class was going to be reading these documents and letters on the Federalist papers as well as letters from Thomas Jefferson to George Washington. I knew what I was getting into. I wanted to take the course because I wanted to see who my enemy was. I wanted to know the problems. I wanted to understand. I wanted to understand the historical figures that so many people in America love. But I also was not going to shut up about it.

At one point, the professor started talking about how Thomas Jefferson actually didn't like slavery, but he was afraid that it would cause financial issues to free the slaves. I was like, great. So I started kind of pushing back, "No, he was racist!" and "No, he thought Black people were inferior to white people. He says that. He says it explicitly." So I was arguing back with him, and the professor was like, "No, you're twisting his words. He's actually saying something else." Then the professor asked, "What does the rest of the class think?" Well, that's not helpful because what are 13 white men going to think? Of course, they defended him! It was me and one other person of color. The two of us are just like, "What?" That professor definitely got tired of me.

I think UVA is an interesting place. If you're in the right bubble, then it's very leftist, it's very progressive. The moment you step outside that bubble, though, it's kind of a free fall. It's a southern school. We forget that sometimes, but it's a southern school. There is quite a big population that would disagree with most things that I just said. I would describe the climate here as outwardly supportive, but in reality it's just a lot of words and no actions. Maybe that's the same for every university. Maybe that's what applies to institutions in general. When August 11th and 12th happened – the *Unite the Right* rally — we asked for a lot of things as students. As student leaders, as people who are involved in the community, we had a lot of demands. None of them were unreasonable. I think they complied with two.

The way that they dealt with student upset and frustration, minority student upset and frustration, was by throwing money into events. They brought Michelle Alexander to speak. She's amazing. I love her. I was happy to see her speak. Her book, *The New Jim Crow,* was great. I want to see her speak. They brought Angela Davis. Of course, I want to see her speak. But they bring people who teach us in their writing and in their speeches to dismantle the very institution at which they're speaking. To dismantle it from the inside out or from the outside in, and UVA is unresponsive. UVA gets angry at our very attempts to do exactly what these speakers tell us to do. That's what frustrates me. I think the climate of UVA is hypocritical. It's very hypocritical. It's so much encouragement and celebration of student work and activism and radicalism, but there's not a willingness to actually make it applicable. It's wild to me that they celebrate by saying, "Our students protest. Our students rally." We're rallying against you. You don't listen!

When Angela Davis was here, I stood up and asked her a question. I was really nervous because all the major UVA leaders were there, but I asked her anyway. I said, "You are teaching us lessons. You are telling us to dismantle the institution, even if we're a part of it. To fight against the forces that are oppressing us, and we want to do that. We are trying. But how do we deal with the fact that you, our role model, was invited and brought in and paid by the very institution that's oppressing us?" People were *shook*! And the question actually got a standing ovation which was wild. The funny part, though, was that there was just this row of UVA administrators who were just sitting down, very stoic. Her answer was to keep on doing it and to remind them of their hypocrisy, which is all we can do. But I'm tired. The climate here is exhausting to students of color. I'm a fourth year student. I can tell you. This whole year, I've just been exhausted. I've had to step back from a lot of leadership roles. Most of them actually. I was really only involved with two organizations this year, which is not a lot for me. I've normally been involved with six or seven. It was taking a toll on my mental and physical well-being.

Last year, I was asked by a fraternity to moderate a dialogue on the history of white supremacy in predominantly white Greek life. I was like, "Okay, they are trying to better themselves. All right, let me do this." So I plan for the whole event, I plan a dialogue, Facebook page, everything. The whole shebang. Five hours before the event, the vice-president of the fraternity, who was my friend and Latinx—it's relevant to the story—texts me and goes, "Hey, we have a problem." Basically, the president of the fraternity, who had not been involved in the process at all, had really not checked in, suddenly checked the Facebook page. He saw the event description and was unhappy. He asked why it is the history of white supremacy in just predominately white Greek life. Why not in all Greek life, including multicultural and Black Greek life? My friend was like, "We can't do that; that's not a thing. Multicultural and Black Greek life was started because non-white students were not admitted to white fraternities and sororities. That's the whole point of this dialogue, that we have a racism problem that still exists. We need to solve it."

Basically, the president said "No," that he's not okay with it. It's a form of defamation or whatever. He said that we needed to change the Facebook page event to say that everyone's going to be present, including multicultural and Black frats and sororities. There are two issues with that. One, they had not been invited outwardly, so you can't change that description a few hours before the event when you know that none of them are going to be there. Two, there's no such thing as a dialogue where people talk about the history of white supremacy in Black and multicultural Greek life; it doesn't make sense. So the guy is saying, "No, that there's also reverse racism. There's reverse racism where they don't let white people into their frats, and there's also racism within their communities." I was like, "You know, there is racism within our communities. None of your business though. We're not gonna discuss that with white people. That's our discussions to have amongst ourselves."

So this guy is pulling this stunt at the last minute. I'm really annoyed.

I have an essay due. I'm trying to write my essay. He's trying to get me to change the event. I text my friend, and I say, "Listen. One, I'm not changing the event. I'd rather cancel it." Then I said, "I was not going to let the 'fraternity president' tell me how to do my job. I have been the *Sustained Dialogue* moderator for, like, three years. This event is happening or it's not." Only I used much more graphic language to describe "the fraternity president." My friend takes a screenshot and unintentionally–he meant to send it to just one of his friends through a GroupMe—sends it to the whole fraternity group chat. The president sees what I said. We cancel the event because he's mad. I was like okay, I don't care. You're the one who does not want to talk about racism in your community. It's not my responsibility to solve white people's racism, so I'm just like, whatever.

Then, the president reports me to the Dean for my language.

Yes, I was reported. I get this email telling me that I need to come in and have a conversation with the head Dean of Sorority and Fraternity life. That they're also bringing in someone from the Office of Diversity and Equal Opportunity to be present for the conversation. I freaked out. I had worked with UJC for a year. I knew that emails that say, "We want to just get your side of the story" could also mean we're getting information for a case. I was like, "What is happening? Am I going to have a UJC case against me because I called someone a graphic name? Are you kidding me?" There was no UJC case when someone called me a terrorist. There was no UJC case when someone called my friend the "N-word."

This is why this incident is such a UVA moment for me.

At the same time that this was happening, Dean Vicki Gist, the Multicultural Student Center (MSC) Dean, found out about it. She was checking up on my file. I don't even know why. I think she just likes to make sure that I'm doing okay because she knows that I be getting myself into situations. She was checking my file, found this case. She contacted the Dean for me. She calls a lot of people and explains to them why this is a ridiculous situation. She tells them that it was not okay. That it's not a good look for them or the school. Basically, she defends me for the whole week leading up to my meeting. By the time I get to the meeting, she's already told me that they're not going to take this to UJC. At this point, they really did just want my side of the story. I went to this meeting and, thanks to her, the Dean who's the head of Sorority and Fraternity Life is apologetic to me. He just wants to hear my story. I tell him my side, also mentioning that he's running a racist institution. I told him, "You have a lot of problems. You're sitting here talking with me about this crap; meanwhile your fraternities are calling black women ugly monkeys when they try to get into parties and using the N-word casually." I just listed off a bunch of stuff that I had heard about and seen. He was like, "Yes, thank you so much for coming in." He was all thankful and apologetic. Honestly, at that point, it was just funny to me. I was too tired to be mad. I just kept thinking that this is ridiculous.

That's why this incident is such a UVA moment for me. It was a moment where I found my allyship with people who supported me, my friend, and the Dean of MSC. I even advocated for myself and told the head of Fraternity and Sorority Life what I was really thinking. I was also in the midst of this ridiculous situation with ridiculous white students who could not have a decent conversation about race and could not understand the nuances. It took that emotional labor out of me. It was just everything all at once. I believe that that's the experience of a lot of minority students at UVA to some degree: you're advocating for one thing, defending yourself against another thing while being attacked by something else but also having someone else rise to defend you. There are good sides and there are also really bad sides.

M.B.

There's a lot of well-intentioned people here in UVA who perhaps don't have the understanding that they think they do, especially when it comes to the typical daily lifestyle of a Muslim student compared to their own. I think people, when they look at me as a hijabi, can tell immediately I'm Muslim. Yet they don't actually know what that means. I guess one example I always think about is how shocked people get when I tell them that I don't drink. I don't do drugs. I feel like typically that's received well. Then other times, I guess in our generation in general, those kinds of religious values aren't necessarily upheld by most people or believed. In a sense, people don't think we should take it seriously. They say, "What's a little sip here?" or "What's a little try there?" I think most people are well-intentioned, but don't necessarily take the time out of their day to look into ways to make Muslims more comfortable or ask the right types of questions, things like that.

Mazzen Shalaby
Class of 2020
College of Arts and Sciences

As an everyday Muslim, someone who's on the Muslim Student Association (MSA) Council for last two and a half years, my overall experiences have been positive. People are overwhelmingly supportive of Islam, of the MSA, of my independent choices as a Muslim. People have been overall respectful on small things, like me not drinking and other bigger issues in college. As with anywhere, I would say there's a lot of ignorance. I don't think it's malicious ignorance, for the most part. There's definitely a lot of problems here too. I've had professors in the past who constantly tie Islam to terrorism or other problematic things. They were not always fully knowledgeable about subjects they're talking about concerning Islam. There have been plenty of problematic things done and said to me. In my first year, somebody posted flyers around the new dorms that said "Terrorist" on the door of a hijabi girl who was active in the community. I know that, unfortunately, MSA members, especially the women who wear hijabs, face constant harassment. So, I don't know. I would say it's majority positive, but unfortunately the loud minority have the ability to spoil it.

People's only exposure to Islam is usually pop culture, school, 9/11, and the "War on Terror." People will learn the textbook definition of what Islam believes but that's about it. People who actually learn anything else are still just constantly bombarded with the media associating Islam with terrorism and Sharia Law. That's where most ignorance comes from. It's not necessarily an unwillingness. I just think it's almost just a lack of opportunity. In my own experience, I've also had the privilege of making a lot of friends and interacting with a lot of people who are very open-minded and bright people. They have a curiosity and want to learn. "Oh, I had no idea about this. Tell me about Islam. Why do you do this?" They have a genuine curiosity and interest in learning and expanding their horizons. I think that if given the opportunity, people will be willing to learn but they're not going to necessarily seek out that opportunity. On a personal level, I think I have tried to make it somewhat the ambition of MSA to educate people about Islam. I'm not shy about practicing Islam, about explaining why I do what I do to people because people don't have the opportunity a lot of time to learn about the religion. I do feel an obligation or duty as a practicing Muslim at UVA to try and educate other people about it. I don't try to be the face of Islam, but for a lot of people, I am the only "Islam" that they interact with on a daily basis, that they know about.

"CARRYING THE BURDEN OF PROMOTING DIVERSITY AND INCLUSION LITERALLY MEANS THAT WE CAN'T INVEST OUR TIME ELSEWHERE"

Rawan Osman
Class of 2022
School of Engineering and Applied Sciences

Rawan Osman's narrative initiates a consideration of the unfair burden placed upon Muslim students to speak out for their community in response to a lack of support from UVA administration and faculty. Osman discusses how being visibly Black, but having her Muslim identity be "invisible," has led to uncomfortable classroom situations. Building on this narrative, Muslim students at UVA discuss the difficulty of finding supportive spaces to discuss the issues faced while being on-Grounds.

YouTube has recommendations as soon as you open your page. Every time I open *YouTube* in the Engineering School, I'm scared that someone will see the recommendations of videos that suggest my faith. I feel like they'll stereotype me, have those negative perceptions of me. I feel that they'll distance themselves from me. I feel like they'll be scared of me because I'm Muslim, which is a terrible thought. There's the deeply entrenched and dangerous stereotype of Muslims as terrorists. I fear the consequences of others' ignorance, of just "not knowing," which is partly a result of misrepresentation through the media. A result of the fact that the media only talks about negative representations of Islam, like 9/11.

I think part of the reason why I'm so uncomfortable is because in elementary school and middle school, we would talk about 9/11 a lot. We would talk about the Muslim identity, but it was always a very shallow conversation. Those conversations made me be afraid to share the fact that I'm Muslim because I come from a pretty predominantly white area where the community is pretty ignorant there about such issues. People definitely don't reach out for information. I'm not sure, though, how I feel about that because there's a lot of things we're all ignorant about that we don't necessarily look into to learn more. So it might be hard to know about some things unless it gets brought to us, though, but I don't think that it justifies ignorance.

The Muslim Student Association (MSA) and The Muslim Institute for Leadership and Empowerment (MILE) are the two spaces where I feel like I can talk about Muslim identity openly as well as in some Black spaces. For instance, we were just talking about our experiences on the whole about being marginalized students. I feel comfortable discussing it there. I'm very, very grateful for those spaces because they are the only places that feel particularly safe talking about my identity in that aspect.

Coming into first year, I don't believe that my being Muslim affected my perception that much. The parts of my identity that did affect my perception are being Black, considering August 11th and 12th. Being female also affected my perceptions of Grounds' safety, knowing about issues of sexual harassment and places to avoid, like Rugby Road. My Black and feminine identity had more effect than my Muslim identity, partly because I don't wear a hijab. People don't have to know I'm Muslim unless I tell them. They will, however, know that I'm Black and that I'm a female immediately, as that's my perceived identity.

I'm treated a certain way based on that initial judgement. People just see me as a Black female, initially. They don't take the time to recognize, "Oh, Rawan might have a lot of talents," or "Rawan might actually be thoughtful and can be intelligent and hold scholarly discussions." They don't think that I'm capable of some type of achievement. It relates to how people think that some students are brought in just for Affirmative Action reasons—the idea that you're not actually as knowledgeable or capable but the institution just needs a Black student to be here for diversity, which is entirely false.

I had a couple negative interactions with faculty members that really highlight this point. There was a particular professor. I felt very strongly that the professor was treating me differently than other females who were white as well as differently from the males in the class. I never brought it up to him. I didn't even know how to go about that. However, I definitely felt like he was not treating me very fairly compared to the rest. I noted how open and friendly he was with other students in particular, but not with me. I also had another interaction with a white man who also works in the engineering school. I went to talk with him regarding my computer. I don't feel comfortable sharing the details of what he said, but some of it very clearly showed me that he just saw me as a Black female. It showed his belief that he could mistreat me or treat me differently than someone else.

There definitely have been things I felt in class that have made me uncomfortable, too, in terms of interactions with students. I can definitely go talk to someone in the Center of Diversity in Engineering about how I feel, how this group project is negatively affecting me and how I'm noticing microaggressions. I don't, however, feel that I can talk to my white professor in class about the microaggressions that I'm feeling. So, I feel like just having someone who understands you is really nice. I definitely have to give credit to my first year Computer Science professor, James Cahoon. He very actively tries to support women in engineering and Computer Science and people of color in Computer Science. He reached out to me and made sure I was comfortable. Besides that one professor and those in the Center for Diversity in Engineering, however, I don't feel like I could talk to any of my other professors about such issues. I definitely would not feel comfortable talking to them about how I'm feeling. There are times that I almost wanted to talk to them, but I was like, "I don't think they're even going to understand." Therefore, my best resources when it comes to talking about microaggressions and issues of that sort are primarily outside of the Engineering school. People like Jannatul Pramanik in the Multicultural Student Center, other Muslim students, and students of color. In terms of faculty, there are probably three people in the entirety of E-School that I can talk to about such things right now.

There is one incident that always comes to mind when asked about my UVA experience. The interaction hugely marred my first year because of how I was treated due to my race. It was December. There was a march that day for Danye Jones, a Black man who was lynched in Missouri. Everyone who went to the march wore all black, so I was wearing all black as well. After the march was over, I went to Runk Dining Hall by myself to get a meal. I didn't think much of it at first, but there was a group of all white students sitting at a table. They got really silent when I walked up past their table. I noticed their stares and silence, but I told myself that I was not going to think much about it. I got my food then sat back down at a table near their table. They started talking about the march but in a very harassing manner. The aggression in their tones and the things that they were saying, like the march being irrelevant, all felt very clearly directed to make me feel uncomfortable. In the moment that it was happening, I kept telling myself, "I'm not going to let y'all get to me." But then the next day, it really struck a nerve. It made me very upset. Until now, when I think of UVA, that's one of the things at the forefront of my mind.

There's a lot of engagement at UVA, but both in a good and a bad way. Social activism, in my perspective, is a big way that students get involved at UVA. It's great. I see a lot of people engaged in social activism. I really respect it. For example, people working at the NAACP, people who are peer advisers with the Office of African American Affairs, MILE, and Latin Leadership

Institute (LLI) are all forms of UVA engagement. I think that they're all spectacular. People really try to put themselves out there to grow and to be part of something important.

Regarding the issue of student self-governance at UVA, first, in the name of full transparency, I was part of Honor first year, but I stopped because I felt like that's something I didn't want to continue. While I was with Honor though, they made a point that I really liked: For those students reported to Honor, they'll either have students who understand the student experience currently trying their case and guiding them through the process or they're going to have a 40 or 50-year-old admin who is much more removed from the student experience making judgments on whether or not they stay at this university. These scenarios are in accordance with and without the presence of student self-governance respectively. Personally, I would rather have a student who is probably more understanding to make that judgment than an administration official.

Even so, student self-governance and these organizations are not without their flaws. First, there's so much responsibility on student and we're definitely not paid or compensated enough for the amount of work and effort it demands. Second, all students are not fairly represented in these organizations. For instance, there's a very recognized issue of spotlighting in Honor. Spotlighting in the sense that students of a certain demography are reported more often than other students. Only 7% of the UVA population is Black, but there's a higher percentage of Black students who go through the Honor system. International students and athletes are also among those who get reported to Honor a lot more often. Therefore, the fact that of those students who go through the system, minorities and athletes are overrepresented, even though numerically they don't make the bulk of the student population, is clearly a problem within all of UVA and a reflection of bias.

Moreover, when I was part of Honor last year, it was not diverse. There definitely was not that many Muslim students, or that many Black students, or people of color. Honestly, it really was not diverse at all! There was the Diversity Committee. It was three or four people, and it was all people who were from minority backgrounds. I just hated that! I felt like they made a Diversity Committee and put the work of that committee on the very small handful of people who are marginalized to try to work on diversity initiatives. Then, the majority of them, who are white, want to work on the policy and the formalities and don't care to be involved in aspects about diversity or inclusion at all. It just felt very fake. The Diversity Committee within Honor felt so fake to me. The people who were in the committee had good things in mind and wanted to do good things, but I didn't respect the fact that for the majority of people in Honor, the Diversity committee was not an effort they wanted to take part in. It felt like the Diversity committee was not considered important by most of them—it wasn't the "prestigious thing," the thing that people wanted to do.

I'm speaking of Honor because that was something that I interacted with very personally. However, I can see this lack in diversity or personal involvement in promoting inclusion by white people with other organizations as well. It's kind of crazy because our values are different. For instance, I'm very involved in social activism and supporting marginalized students because I know how painful it can be to be Muslim or a Black female at UVA, so I invest a lot of my time in that. As a result, I feel like I can't put my efforts elsewhere! Other people, however, don't have to think about parts of their identity like that, so they don't invest time in it. It's like the things that I have to think about on a daily basis, they don't even have to think about at all. This is why it's a problem when the issues of representing Muslim students or other students of marginalized background only falls on Muslims or those marginalized communities—because this burden literally means that we can't invest our time elsewhere! Therefore, it shouldn't be only on us to promote diversity and inclusion. That's what leads to, for example, racial battle fatigue.

Before I say what UVA can do better or differently to help students like me, I want to talk about a certain interaction that I had with an older white man. I was at dinner, and we were all discussing climate change. That dinner was the day of the March for Climate Change and Awareness at the Rotunda. I was telling this man about the marches that were happening in Charlottesville and around the US, about the issues of climate change. He legitimately was scoffing at what I was saying. He was kind of laughing. I could tell he didn't believe me. He thought, "Oh, this is just a young person making up problems. She's just trying to have something to talk about." He didn't give me any credibility in what I was saying. It made me feel like we're just viewed as young people without credibility, and so our problems aren't taken seriously.

Therefore, I wish that the administrators of UVA would take us more seriously and would not be so reluctant to the changes that we ask. I wish that they were willing to be a bit more radical in the way that they change things. Like I was saying about Honor. It was established long ago, and change is happening far too slowly, partly because even people who are students here now don't want to be involved in issues of diversity and inclusion or don't believe there's a problem. I hope this publication gets to the right people at UVA administration, that they really take it seriously, and try to make Muslim students and other marginalized students feel more comfortable here. And not just on a surface level, just to say that they did something. I hope that they deeply try to institute change!

K.G.

If I can say something for any student, and specifically minority students: Although it may seem that you exist in a hostile space, in a space where you're deemed as "the Other" wherever you go, I hope it doesn't discourage anybody from finding the space in which they can make an impact, they can express their views, where they can advocate for a particular belief that they have, and to stand behind that belief.

This university, with all of its glaring flaws, has plenty of different ways in which a student who's passionate about something can get involved and make their voice heard whether people want to hear it or not. It can be very discouraging every day when you have to deal with all these issues of class, of race, of hierarchies that inevitably exist. With that said, I think every student can figure out how they can use that frustration, use that passion, use that knowledge that they're gaining from their courses, from their experiences, and then figure out where they can have a say on the future of this university. In order to make it better for the students that come after you and for the students that are going to be here 20 or 30 years from now, it's on every student here to make their voice heard, to stand by their beliefs even when you're going to face blowback, when people might not want to hear it.

I definitely believe, though, that this work puts a lot of pressure on minority students because white students don't exactly have to fight for their "privileges." But minority students, for them to be acknowledged the way that they are, what they go through, their experiences, and their needs, I'm saying, they have to put in effort to be recognized. I think it's a systematic and unfair balance of power that essentially puts all of that weight on and forces minority students to bear the brunt of fighting for some of the same fundamental experiences that white students enjoy on a daily basis that they may not be aware that they enjoy. That's the age-old history of this country, of colonialism, that has shaped power dynamics between white people, people of color, and religious minorities, that has made minorities have to shoulder that burden.

I think the positive is that minorities, at least, are in control of their narrative. It doesn't leave any room for others to redefine or shape, in any way, what that narrative looks like. I think it's the minorities' narrative to tell, and then through their involvement, through their time at the university, figuring out the best way to put that forward. That's what I mean by finding the space that you are comfortable in and that you are able to push your passions. In those spaces, you're going to interact with students who are not aware of how such work is exhausting for a minority student. Through those interactions, through the work that you're doing, you can get them to be an ally in that process. This will take some of that burden off so that you really don't feel like it's "us versus them" this entire time. Slowly, over time, it can become a collective effort to remedy some of those issues. Right now, it is a very unequal spread of the burden. It is, unfortunately, shouldered by minorities.

Sara Ali
Class of 2021
College of Arts and Sciences
Class of 2022
McIntire School of Commerce

Everyone knows the stereotype of UVA college. Everyone here is very competitive. I wouldn't say it's a very helpful environment. I've been here about two years, creeping up on two and a half, and people don't talk about their mistakes. People don't talk about a bad grade. You just keep everything to yourself, which is so unhealthy because the people who do good, they voice their goodness, and it's great. You want to be happy for your friends, and you are. But it's to a point now where it's only people who are doing good who have a voice. So, you think everyone else is doing good when in reality, there are other people struggling like you, whether it's with homework or something that happened to you. Whatever it is, sometimes you're just too afraid to speak up, you know?

I do think that UVA wants to help. They have programs for first-generation and low-income students. They have these talks. They have these meetings. But I think it's too professional. It's not one of those laid-back things I could go to. I wish I could have come here to UVA and have found a group of people who were exactly like me, in the sense that they were low-income, they were the first-generation. I think having that group of people that were from back home, I could easily talk about my problems. They would have been on the same track as me when we can talk about our problems. They could relate to the problems. They wouldn't have taken in the competitive environment that is UVA. Not having those people has shaped me and molded me to fit the rest of UVA, becoming silent in my struggles, becoming somewhat competitive, and not wanting to voice any bad things about me, you know? Yeah.

The UVA community, in a way, despises vulnerability. It's weird, that word "vulnerability." It was something we learned in high school. We learned these generic phrase of "You have to fail to succeed." We took that in high school, and we understood. They taught us this word and they said, "You'll carry this throughout the rest of your life." But then you come to a place where that word is completely diminished, where they expect you to be on top of everything at 110%. Hearing that word is so shocking because it's like,

"Wow" I haven't heard that since high school." It's so interesting. It's like, "Wait, I used to have that. Being vulnerable. That used to be me." Now I'm just the UVA student and everything that embodies.

I.F.

One of the things with religion, and social atmospheres in general, is the stigma around mental health. So especially coming into college, that's a pretty big issue that literally every campus has to deal with. The first week on campus, I feel like UVA really emphasized it a lot. They're like, "Oh, if you need help, go get help. We're here for you." After that, it's just like, "Just go with it." There's still kind of a weird stigma around it. I feel like if you're vulnerable, you're not contributing as much to UVA's goals as a school. They do have a lot of options for students who want to talk about their issues, but there's still just a stigma with reaching out in general. This is especially true if you think about it from a religious standpoint. A lot of cultures do not believe mental illness is a thing. They think it's a completely American concept, even though it's not. But they think the rates are because of America's advertising of services, like it's like an industry here. For someone who grows up in an environment where you're not expected to be mentally ill even if you are, you have to just kind of play it off. Coming here and still seeking out those resources is quite hard.

"I CAN'T BELIEVE THAT CAME OUT OF YOUR MOUTH"

Ilyas Saltani
Class of 2022
College of Arts and Sciences

Ilyas Saltani's narrative initiates a consideration of the role of student activism in creating a safe environment for all students. Through his narrative, Saltani articulates the way power is structured between the student body and the academy. He notes how activism at UVA is more performative than actual. That the administration will often "throw money at problems" instead of getting to the root of the issue. Expanding on Saltani's analysis, Muslim students at UVA then highlight how this power structure affects their ability to engage the university on important issues within their community.

When I came to UVA, I already had a notion of the university being a predominantly white institution, a narrative many BIPOC students and students from marginalized backgrounds comprehend in their own way. For this reason, I didn't come in with any expectations that my background or interests would be widely shared or accepted. Establishing this early helped alleviate some of the burdens of navigating this university, but you often get reminded of your identity and "Otherness" quite frequently.

As it pertains to my identity, there are many different ways that people can represent Islam and their adherence to the religion both outwardly, and even within, Muslim spaces. I think I hold a lot of privilege in the sense that I am not "visibly" Muslim at first sight. It's important to recognize the harm many Muslims endure for wearing a hijab or any other religious and/or cultural signifiers that are often weaponized against them. This was a privilege I carried too proudly when I first came to UVA, as I felt that an aspect of finding community at this school was masking the parts of my identity that did not align with the status quo. In hindsight, not only was this problematic across many different fronts but worse, it complicated my own relationship with Islam as I began to internalize this resentment which took even longer to unlearn. I very quickly began to witness the Islamophobia that permeated many different spaces. These were things I experienced personally from being a resident in on-Grounds housing to a resident advisor (RA) and student leader in various organizations, and even just as another student looking at it from a third-person perspective.

There are also students that are typically affiliated with political alignments that may be inherently opposed to Islamic values and who will publicly and very boldly demonize Islam. I'm in the "What's the Move" chat, a large GroupMe with about 2000 students that typically advertise progressive ideas, events, and forums that are happening around the Grounds. However, every so often there will be a member who makes a bold statement in an attempt to "challenge" perspectives without realizing the harm they cause. For example, when we were advertising for the Muslim Institute for Leadership and Empowerment this semester, there was a student who responded to our blurb with something derogatory. It was obviously directed towards the idea of Muslim leadership, wanting to silence that notion as though Muslim leaders are a scary thing to have on-Grounds. I and some others quickly chimed in to explain why that statement was wrong and harmful. He ended up just leaving the chat. He didn't want to have any positive discourse about it. He didn't want to have a discussion to better understand our feelings about the issue. He just left.

I feel like that, in itself, is representative of the whole narrative about challenging discourse at UVA. It is not a discussion that is wanted because individuals are comfortable in their privilege and are guided by preconceived notions that don't require them to interrogate the impact of their own identities. I've seen and heard a lot of instances where people are convinced that Islam is inherently a religion of hate. That Islam is a religion that marginalizes women, queer people, or other identities. While I am a progressive Muslim, having my own understanding of how I want to practice Islam. I will be the first to advocate that it's not true though I also can't ignore the ways many people in my community have weaponized the religion to marginalize communities for their own interests, though this is not representative of the entire Muslim world.

Circling back to a previous discussion, I had been through that phase I think many Muslim-Americans experience where I questioned my religion just because of everything that you see on the internet, the media, and how it's portrayed. You feel like you want to create this "us versus them" dynamic — that I'm not like "them." At a time where many people don't really understand the values of your religion or the purpose of religion in general, you're just like, "It's easier to just not associate with that." It was a harmful thing to go through, but I think it was an essential component of my personal growth that helped refine my stances and identity. You begin to appreciate the religion a lot more, and the values that it truly stands for. You understand that it's not about regurgitating principle, but it's how you interpret those principles and channel them into your daily life to be a good person.

When I'm with Muslim friends, I say things like, "Insha'Allah" in passing conversation. Whenever I'm with non-Muslim people, then I suddenly put up a front, and I find myself suppressing certain cultural signifiers. That's where it becomes difficult in grappling with your identity, trying to figure out who you are. I feel like as long as you're able to hold on to your principles and your values without losing them, you are okay. There is a fine line between being fake and just being understanding of the crowd that you're with at that moment — code-switching, if you will. I'm willing to be respectful and conservative with my ideas with certain people while still holding onto what I believe in and projecting it slightly on both sides, being very conscious of the way I navigate both spaces.

I think the first thing that people notice is that I'm not just "a white American." It definitely does influence the way that you're treated. Like professors, for example. I was applying for research positions in my first year. This one professor asked for an interview. I met with him. It went horribly because he ended it within, like, five minutes, which was weird because I usually do fine in interviews. Then I began to realize that I wasn't what he was looking for in a hire because his lab looked very homogenous in terms of demographics. I ended up getting a position in another lab, funny enough, literally across the hall from him. They're all white. I mean, I'm not going to be the one to say that that was the reason, but you know, it's like, if the shoe fits. He has an implicit idea of what he thinks people who look like me are about. He just wasn't going to associate with that.

Another instance. I took the Intro to Global Studies: Middle East/South Asian class during my first semester here. That class, honestly, was one of the classes, if not the class, that defined my college trajectory. I established a really amazing relationship with Professor Tessa Farmer. I also determined that this was sort of the route of study that I wanted to follow. Yes, I'm Pre-Med but not everything has to be bio-medically driven. This was the class where Islam was the most ingrained. It was a small class. I was one of two Muslim students because everybody else was white. It would be funny because you would be talking about these issues, and, as a Muslim student, you would want to exhibit that, be like, "As a Muslim student, here's what I think about this based on my experiences." This might make it more personable. Then at that point, you're branded as like the token Muslim student in the class that everybody would turn to when they can't answer something or for confirmation. I don't know why certain people of privilege like to think that they're not qualified to talk about certain things. I think to a degree you may not know enough, but you're always qualified to have that conversation. Their favorite thing to say, though, is "Oh, I'm not qualified to talk about this topic." Then they defer to me or the other Muslim student in the class as sort of the cop-out. I'm like, "You know, part of the purpose here is that you're taking this class so that you can become more qualified to talk about these things, and if you're just going to keep deferring to the Muslim student to uphold these understandings, it's not really doing anything for you."

You begin to realize these power structures in terms of what is considered hegemonic and what is not. It's interesting because as a Muslim, you feel that a lot of your views are questioned when you notice that many views in Christianity, or Catholicism, or Judaism, while they may be criticized, are not questioned or are not delegitimized at the same scale that Muslim values are, even though, for the most part, many of them exhibit a lot of parallels. I find it is emotionally taxing to have to defend things, to have to continue to justify yourself. And it's not a matter of "Oh, let me prove to you why." They come in with the understanding that they're looking for something to be wrong, so they want you to defend it, so that you can prove to them that it's not. It's a tricky ground because, well, I'm tired of playing that role. Can you do it yourself? Can you open your mind yourself?

I think ignorance is definitely a fundamental reason, but I feel like it's just media perception at this point. This is how they've been trained to think about Islam. Islam has become equitable to many things that are negative in the media. It's just a matter of revalidation. It's a matter of telling them, "Here's why what you heard about this particular instance is not true. Here's where this has been exaggerated. Here's why Muslims are marginalized." But it's hard to envision somebody who *is* in a position of privilege as not being in a position of privilege when you're looking at them from a third person viewpoint. That's how I guess it seems for people when they're looking at Islam. All they're seeing and understanding about Islam is negativity. It's hard for them to imagine it as anything else unless you show them empirical concrete reasons as to why it's not. To say that it's ignorant is miss of the many other reasons that these conversations are not happening the way they should be. Yes, people may not understand. That's a component, but it's also not wanting to understand. There's a barrier there too. It's a two-way street because you can explain as much as you want, but if someone is not receptive to that, you can only go so far.

The more time that I spend here, and the more minority spaces that I occupy and see how they're treated, the more I begin to realize that there is so much wrong with this university. It's really funny because I always try to see the best in things. I like to think, "It's all going to be okay. They're trying their best. Look at all these initiatives, look at all this money that is being put towards students who are marginalized." But when you look into it more, you realize there is a whole network of just wrong-doing and immoral acts. I could talk about it for days. It's so problematic. For example, I was a student Council Representative. Last semester there was a petition that had gone out about the only professor of color in the Global Studies department whose contract was not being renewed. It's the Global Studies department, and you have one professor of color who can share those experiences. The professors are informed as to why their renewal is not happening. But for her, there was no reason. She didn't even know. It was really confusing. She was an advocate for women, women's sexuality, gender dynamics, religion, just colors and issues within the Global Studies department. She was really qualified to have those discussions, more so than other white professors could even if they tried. It was just a huge loss to no longer have her.

So I decided, as a representative with a platform, I'm going to share the concerns that the students are raising with the petition. I'm going to help circulate it. I'm going to do a little bit of investigating on my own to see what we can do or why it's happening. I met with administrators. I met with the Dean of Diversity and Inclusion. There was definitely something going on. We have never been able to find out the full reason. They would never tell us. Certain deans refused to talk about her case because I didn't have "any legal reason to know" and they could not legally share any information with me. I thought, "Okay, so perfect." That's when it hit me. I realized, "So this is what UVA does, like this is how it is." They will go to lengths to not talk about what they don't want the public to see. I believe there probably was information they could legally share, but if not sharing is at the expense of minority professors having public allies, then so be it. That viewpoint was validated for me because an administration figure, someone high up who I was speaking to about diversity and inclusion literally told me, "I'd rather have a room of white men who are competent than a single token colored professor." I was like, "Oh, interesting." I wrote it word for word because I was like "I can't believe that came out of your mouth." There's still no replacement. Her position is still not filled. I just thought, "Okay, so this is what it's about," and the deeper that I get involved, the more I see it.

Think about it from our perspective. Actually, not only in terms of Muslim students, but just people of color, Black people, people who look Muslim, it may not even be due to their religion, but it's due to that part of the world that they come from. No matter how much we'd like to say that we are equitable, they're not treated the same. If you want to talk about having competent white professors, and you want to create this culture that sort of allows people to feel comfortable here, you're not going to do it by then setting the example of the one Brown professor in Global Studies being let go. Looking at it as a professor of color who wants to come and work at this university, who wants to come and share their knowledge, they're not going to see these examples because it was swept under the rug. But how does it look? The optics that it creates in terms of how these professors and people are treated, it's just problematic, frankly. That's why I thought that, "I can't let this narrative get swept under the rug because she's just going to be another professor that's forgotten." Her story is never going to be told. Nothing is going to change. It needs to be something that's elucidated.

In that way, I don't think there is any concrete thing that can be done to really make me feel more comfortable here. I think UVA and this college community need to realize that throwing money at certain initiatives or certain groups of people is not going to solve their problems. It's not going to make us feel any more welcome in this space. I realize it's not going to happen overnight or even over a year. I think that it is a decade long plus procedure. It involves switching your mindset to better understand and a lot of people just don't get it. This can be applied to so many of the issues that I see. Think of the first-gen students who are still fighting for representation at this university. Of course, people who don't think they're deserving of that will be like, "Well, President Ryan has commissioned a hundred million dollars towards you." You can throw money at them all you want, but it's how you *feel* at this university, how you wake up in the morning, and then you realize your space, and how you occupy it, that is much different than how somebody else does.

It's like this watchlist for example. I'm talking about the culture that it creates. It's not about the money. The argument for having it is, "Oh, why not award donors who give millions of dollars to this university to provide opportunities to students, their children, the chance to be matriculated?" It's the very practice of that watchlist that is the issue because you will wake up in the morning as a first-gen student, as a low-income student, as a minority student, and know that you are never going to be on that list. You will never be able to put your kids on that list because you're just not privileged in that way. You are just never going to end up with that sort of privilege. That is just not how you were born. That sort of dichotomy where you're letting those types of students in at a much lower threshold. Like they are here, they have a spot in this university because their parents paid for them while somebody else who is coming from a low economic background is working so hard to get accepted. Somebody was saying that this is how it is in the real world. It's like, "Yeah, that's how it is in the real world because you, and other people like you, are products of institutions like this one who are taking these practices into the real world. Nothing is going to change. It's going to create a cycle." We need to set a precedent. Stop it before it continues. It's okay to lose donors.

As a student representative, if I see something that is detrimental to the student body, that marginalizes a particular group, I want it abolished. I don't care how the university makes money. I really feel like money is now just a cop-out. "Oh, they have money, so they're fine." Or "Oh, there's no funding for this, so let's just trash it." It's all about money. I think we're way too dependent on it. We're not realizing the emotional, socio-emotional aspects that it creates for students. If we want them to feel like they are welcome in this space, it's adjusting that environment as opposed to just throwing money at them. I wish that the administration and the campus climate would understand. I realize that a lot of these issues are not just Muslim. They're intersectional. It's being Muslim and Black. It's being Muslim and first-gen. It's not having privilege. It's a lot of other things. You can't just talk about one identity and ignore the rest. All these identities are intertwined, and their experiences at UVA are all related.

Overall, I am so happy and proud to see Muslim representation. We have so many Muslim RAs. We have the most Muslims in Lawn rooms, in leadership positions, in Student Council. We are starting to have a voice now. We're starting to advocate for ourselves and have an opinion on issues that are influencing our students. A lot of times, when decisions are made, people in the room do not really consider that there are different identities that will respond to different initiatives. Muslim students, who have experienced a level of marginalization, in that sense, can advocate for marginalized communities. No matter how much you study it in a vacuum, as a white student, you won't get the socio-emotional aspect of that experience. It's not something that you can learn or read about. It's something that you *feel*. A lot of times, it's even indescribable. It's understanding social cues or mannerisms in ways that you interact and engage with other people that makes you *feel* marginalized. There are things that you just won't understand unless you've experienced them. Being able to vocalize that in a larger space and having the platform to advocate for your people in that way is huge. I'm still proud of our community for being able to do that. It's inspiring! The first-year incoming Muslims can say, "Someone has already done it, so I can do it too now."

Shahira Ali
Class of 2022
College of Arts and Sciences

I came from a very diverse area in Northern Virginia. My high school was relatively diverse. I always heard that "UVA is a white school," so I was honestly worried before coming here. When I came for orientation, I saw maybe two hijabis, but that was enough to make my mom happy. Then once I actually got here and joined the Muslim Student Association and attended all my classes, I was surprised by the number of Muslims I saw. I appreciate how much more diverse UVA is than I thought it would be in the beginning.

Still more than the presence of Muslims at UVA, I found it valuable to have people understand what it means for me to be Muslim — just be educated about it. I didn't have to constantly explain my values and beliefs to every person I met, meaning I wouldn't have to tell every single person what Islam is, what a hijab is, that I'm Muslim. When my parents visit Grounds, my mom is always looking for the physical representation, I guess. "Oh, do I see a hijabi over here?" But for me, I honestly don't mind as long as the people are open-minded. At UVA, I didn't have to constantly go around telling people like, "Oh yeah, I'm Muslim, I'm hijabi. And that's how this works." People would just either respect it automatically, they already know, or they don't feel like it's something they need to know about. They are not uncomfortable with needing things explained to them. That said, I don't mind explaining my religion or beliefs to people who are genuinely curious.

I just feel like I haven't seen the Muslim Student Association (MSA) really being out there. MSA is MSA, but it's not something that's so UVA. When you think of huge UVA organizations, MSA is a big one. But people automatically look to sororities or other cultural organizations, like the Indian Student Association or Organization of Young Filipino Americans. I feel like the MSA is still not as heavily known as it should be, considering our membership. I honestly don't know why. Maybe we need to advertise more. We need to put ourselves out there more. I also feel like it's UVA, too. Some of UVA's administrators lack the interest to understand and seek MSA out. It's not like, "Oh, I don't want to talk to Muslims." I definitely don't think it's that. I think they just don't feel it's necessary. They think, "Oh, they're already a huge organization. It's fine. We can leave them where they are. It's not going to make that big of a difference if we do engage with them." The administration's priorities are definitely in different areas. They are not necessarily bad priorities, but they are not equally spread out.

I suppose too much engagement can be bad, too. If they were heavily involved in MSA, then people could also take that the wrong way like, "Why are they always trying to figure out what MSA's doing?" See, that's what I'm saying. How people take things. I personally think if they want to know all about MSA and become extremely engaged, I wouldn't mind. I would say, just by looking at the situation, the administration being less involved makes it seem like they may not be that interested, which might be discouraging for some people. Getting recognition is always a good thing so that Muslims know UVA is always looking out for them, too.

Ahmed Hussain
Class of 2023
School of Engineering and Applied Sciences

I think, generally, policies like Affirmative Action are useful, and I support the idea of expanding the demographics of a university. I feel as if a lot of people don't understand the purpose of Affirmative Action. "Why should Affirmative Action be a thing if a person is able to get into a good school without the help of others?" But, if you don't know something is possible, you probably can't achieve it. The reason a person not benefitting from Affirmative Action is able to get their spot in the first place is most likely because other people helped them, whether it's someone who mentored them or someone who understood their background. There are people who take on the role of a support structure to get them there. I guess a politically-relevant term for that would be privilege – many of the groups benefitting from policies like Affirmative Action don't have such privileges.

Fadumo Hussein
Class of 2023
College of Arts and Sciences

My experiences as a Muslim, as a woman, and as a Black person are fundamental, but I think the Alderman Library concern is the tip of the iceberg when it comes to not only student concerns, but our system itself. What does it mean to be at a location that values money over people? How do we challenge harm caused by white supremacy when white supremacy is the foundation? Do we reform? Or do we completely divest and start anew? I don't know.

UVA is very engaged in trying to address these issues, but what's weird is how engagement is done. I feel like if you just don't know the right people, or if you're not in the right societies, or if you're not in the right secret societies, or if your plans seem to conflict with alumni interests, then your plan usually doesn't work out to the extent that you want it to. For example, let's just talk about the Alderman Library. The Black Student Alliance (BSA) wants to change the name of the Alderman Library because while he was the first president of UVA, he was a racist as well as a eugenicist. But if you have alumni who went to this school and want to continue UVA having its "good old tradition" of calling the building the Alderman Library, UVA is going to value alumni because they are what keeps the lights on here. It's a problem because obviously some students in UVA want to make a change so UVA will feel more inclusive.

If you look at it in terms of the bigger picture, you're allowing the libraries to be a way to recognize a UVA president who felt strongly against African Americans and Black people as a whole. You expect students who are Black and African American to feel okay and safe in that environment, to feel that they're fully respected. So, if alumni have a stronger influence on wanting to keep the name, I wouldn't be surprised if it stayed the same. Even though President Jim Ryan is looking into changing it (or at least he has recognized that it is an issue amongst the student body), alumni keep the lights on, so they're going to have more sway. It creates a sense of skepticism. "Oh, do these broader institutions actually work? Does student self-governance really work?" In a perfect world, they wouldn't take money from the alumni. That would make sure if there was a need for change, there wouldn't be so much hesitation, or at least stagnation, in creating those changes. But it comes back to just figuring out where they are going to get the money. It comes back to the issue of who are the stakeholders that have the money and if those stakeholders have beliefs that go against the student body.

"AS A MUSLIM MYSELF, IT SHOULD NOT BE MY RESPONSIBILITY TO FIGURE OUT HOW TO DO IT FOR THEM"

Khadeja Muhammed

Khadeja Muhammad's narrative initiates a consideration of the practices and real-world effects of student self-governance. She discusses the work necessary for students to utilize self-governance to make a difference, "to be the change," by creating spaces in her community as well as other student communities to resist oppressive practices and traditions. Building on her insights, Muslim students at UVA expand this investigation into how students are often burdened by the necessity of doing such work and the necessary role of the administration in addressing student concerns.

Islam at UVA, in other words "the Muslim scene," is one of those things that you have no idea about unless you, yourself, are a Muslim that attends the university. Unless you are thinking about Muslims or have Muslim friends, the things that happen within our community don't really cross your mind at all. I'm taking a class now called "The Muslim Question," and I love it. We get to talk about Islam as an analytical category, not just a religion. I find that really cool. I feel very, very lucky to be in that class because it's a small seminar of maybe 20 students, so not many people will have the opportunity to take it. I think it would be really weird for the university to be like, "Muslims exist on this campus!" but if they're going to say that this institution is welcoming to diverse groups of students, including Muslims, and that it can be a home to them, the university should be taking it upon themselves to actually make sure that's true. I haven't seen that happening necessarily though—not genuinely, sustainably, or meaningfully enough.

As a Muslim myself, it should not be my responsibility to figure out how to do it for them, especially as I am trying to navigate the conditions as they currently exist. Muslim students, POCs, and marginalized students in general, as the people who have experienced the discrimination or oppression, should never have to bear the burden of fixing these issues. At the end of day, we're students who go here just like our white, wealthy, cis-het,

Christian counterparts. If there's a problem with inclusion, then the university needs to take it upon themselves to fix it and make this place more comfortable for students. If the university does not do that, then they're being hypocritical when they advertise, "Record-breaking diverse acceptance numbers." They need to back it up and make sure that those "diverse" students are thriving when they get here too. The university has been exclusive for centuries. If the university is claiming diversity is increasing, then they need to change the campus, change the culture, to fit what they claim with such pride. It's not matching up.

The university also shouldn't expect Muslim students to come share their trauma and share everything that they've been through in hopes of fixing the problem themselves. If the university actually cares, then it needs to listen to grievances of the marginalized, nurture their mental, emotional, social needs, and figure out solutions. Then it needs to spend the money. At the end of the day, it's not fair that Muslim students are having more of the responsibility put on us to do it ourselves after being the ones who were highlighting the issue in the first place. I do think, though, that Muslims need to be the ones voicing their concerns. I don't want a table of all non-Muslims or all white people assuming what the Muslim experience is about, but that also shouldn't be expected. The university should be thankful to have people who want to come out and share their experiences. Then the university should fix the issue based on what those students are saying.

Last year, the Muslim Student Association (MSA) worked on making dining hall accommodations for Muslim students. It is something that obviously most students don't think about, but Muslim students who fast for a month need to be sure to get their money's worth in a different way than students who don't fast. That's something that obviously nobody in administration is going to be thinking about unless you have a Muslim student present. Muslim students have to do that extra work and make their voices heard. I guess it's a fight for the first group of students who do it, but they know that it's going to be better for everyone who comes after them. Still, it shouldn't have to be something that Muslim students have to do on their own and with immense obstacles.

Think about the anti-Muslim flyers from a couple years ago. I think, in a lot of ways, the university believes that sending out an email is going to take care of everything. It's not! The emails show that the university thinks such actions are wrong—that the university shouldn't stand for those things. But an email is a very small thing to do. It doesn't make Muslim students feel that the university actually cares. It feels like they're just checking it off their list, that such emails are things that they need to do just so that it's said, "We did something."

It's really hard to transition into professors talking about Islam in a very academic way, a perspective from which students normally have never heard discussions of Islam. So, the jump for the majority, from everyone's initial understanding of Islam, based on media, to that discussion is kind of daunting for them. I don't think it gets as much care when it's being taught. The classes operate under the assumption that students have a certain level of knowledge about Islam, but they don't have it. It's a really shocking abrupt experience for them. I think that is why students find it frustrating to learn about Islam in classes. Still, professors have the power in these classrooms to say that Muslims aren't terrorists. They can straighten out the misconceptions. However, it would be almost foolish of professors to flat out say, "Muslims aren't terrorists." It's assuming that framework is the understanding to begin the discussion. That, in itself, is problematic. For instance, if in an African American studies class, a professor said, "Oh by the way, Black people aren't drug dealers," everyone is going to be puzzled and be like, "What? There is no need to say that!" It would just be perpetuating the idea that "Black People are drug dealers" is the norm. It's not. I feel like it's very similar to the idea that Muslims aren't terrorists.

Being Black has also undoubtedly shaped and informed my experiences and understandings of power at UVA. I think in the same way that I am a first-generation American, the same way that I am low-income student, it's all the same pattern of being under-represented, of having to fight for my own spaces, fight for my own needs and wants to be acknowledged by the university. The longer that I'm at this university, the more that I am discovering that it is the same root for all these issues. It's different fights, but it all stems from this university being founded on white supremacy, cis-het patriarchy, and capitalism. That's it. That's generally what oppressive, unaccommodating, violent, exclusive structures come down to. I think it became easier once I got to that point, which is very recently, honestly. Even with different communities, everyone thinks that they're experiencing something very different, something very ostracizing and unique. But are they really different? Yes. They're experiencing a different sort of discrimination or different struggle, but it's all the same thing. The roots of our problems are the same!

That insight has made me deeply examine and reflect on my identities.

It was complicated for me to be Black in the MSA and to be Muslim in certain Black spaces. I'm at the point now where these experiences are making me have a more holistic understanding of who I am and what my contributions to this university are going to be. All of my prior experiences have been brought together. They're all mushed together because of similar underlying issues. At the same time, it's encouraged me, even though I shouldn't *have* to, to do certain things, to put my energy towards certain things, to vocalize my opinions. When I was a part of the Organization of African Students, I hosted an event on colorism because that affects multiple different communities. This is an issue, and the university doesn't think about it. They are not even aware that this is an issue because the majority of this institution is white people. They think racism is the extent to which discrimination against skin color happens. There was another event I hosted through the Minority Rights Coalition on Kashmiri, Kurd, and Uyghur Muslims. It focused on the discrimination, violence, and Islamophobia happening across the world. Again, the university is not going to bring speakers to talk about these issues specifically and raise awareness, but student organizers have and will. So I'm just making sure that I'm using the spaces that students created to have those conversations. I know students really want to have those conversations. Muslims will feel more heard and supported. Students from all those groups will feel heard and supported.

What all the moments that I've had at UVA have in common is *resistance*. Given everything that I've talked about so far, I guess this shouldn't be surprising. Coming into UVA, I had a really love/hate relationship with this school for various reasons. As I walk around Grounds, I always see how it's all so beautiful. Then instantly, my next thought is how this ground, and everything on it, was built by enslaved laborers. Coming to terms with how institutions work, as well as understanding that UVA is an institution, requires effort. A lot of back and forth with yourself.

There's just so many things that are wrong with this school: the way the students are affected, the way the Charlottesville community residents are affected by this university and even the way that this university exploits people in prisons. I'm not sure how many students know this, but all the laundry that's done by the UVA hospital is done by a women's prison 30 miles outside of Charlottesville. The women get paid, like, 25 cents an hour. A lot of the furniture on-Grounds is built by people in prison. They're paid, like, 16 cents an hour. This stuff still happens. It's in a contract with the state of Virginia. It's like a Virginia code or something. It's crazy! To this day, 16 cents an hour?! It reminds me of sharecropping. It's exploitation!

Therefore, I think my time at UVA is a combination of resisting against certain things that I don't like and trying to change those things as much as I can before I graduate. I like to help organize different events and join in on the different movements happening on-Grounds, like walkouts, protests, petitions, or hosting events that raise awareness. Furthermore, I want to help in creating spaces for people to discuss issues that they care about because the university is not thinking about those issues. The university is thinking of the average UVA student, which is a white person. I try to figure out how I can make students of color, Muslim students, and marginalized students feel more welcome at this school, and then I help realize that goal. This is the type of work that the university either doesn't care about or is completely oblivious to, both of which are equally disappointing.

UVA does pride itself on student self-governance, but frankly, I think student self-governance is a mind-fuck. First of all, students are tired! All the stuff that students do in the name of student self-governance is what paid professionals do at other schools. It's their livelihood! When you look at the bureaucracy of UVA and how this university works, there's a category of things that paid professionals would do, but it is students that are doing it at UVA. It tricks students into thinking that it's up to students, that the university has no responsibility to make students feel welcome, but it does. If it doesn't make you feel welcomed, then the university should advertise that instead of diversity. If the university actually cared, then it would be taking other measures. At the end of the day, student self-governance is the university ridding itself of responsibility and dumping it on students: "You have the power to do it yourself, so do it yourself." What's more is that the entire student body is not going to contribute to this necessary work; it's going to be done by the few people that are affected by the things that have been messed up for 200 years. Student self-governance can also be really dangerous because it is something that one can use to easily manipulate. It's just really convenient. I don't know if that was the intention from the start. It was really prestigious at the beginning that students did this work, but now it makes it easy for the university. It lets them say that "Students have the power to change things, so they should stop complaining and do something about it." But that shouldn't be our job! There are certain things that shouldn't be students' job when we come here to learn and live as university students.

People are engaged with themselves and people that look like themselves. POC are engaged with each other; all the POC, Latinx students, Black students engage with each other. When I did the Kashmir, Kurd, and Uyghur event, white people were there. I was surprised. I was actually very confused. There were, like, 50 students at the event and around 10 of them were white and I was shocked. I was like, "Are you guys lost?" I didn't say that out loud obviously, but that was my thought. Apparently a professor had told them to come for extra credit. When I learned that fact, their presence made sense. My shock was justifiable. This is what I mean. This is how we know that it's a very small number of students who engage of their own accord with others not considered like themselves. I think white people, being the majority of this university, just need to care more about others and not just themselves. I don't know if that's going to happen, though. People with power in general need to recognize their privilege. They need to recognize that they have a lot of things easier. And until they do, I guess we'll just keep doing this.

Mazzen Shalaby
Class of 2020
College of Arts and Sciences

Student governance is a good thing, overall. I think there's conversations going on now about more support for student leaders. As somebody who's involved with leading a couple of clubs myself, I know it's a huge grind. It's a full-time job on top of being a student, especially if you work as well or do research. It's brutal how much work is involved with these organizations. Burnout is very real. I probably spend more time on club stuff on the average week than I do on academics on certain weeks. And you don't realize how much time you spend on it until you're actually doing the work of it. Maybe that's the reason why if you look at a lot of student councils, nobody comes back for a second year. I was the only one who returned from the MSA Council because a lot of people were tired. They were saying, "I'm cooked from my year on Council." Same thing the year before that. I think nobody came back. And that's true of a lot of organizations that people just get toasted for the year. So, in terms of student self-governance, I think there should be more support from the university for leaders. And that support should be more explicit so that the burden isn't all on the students, especially for minority students, for underprivileged students. If you have to work a full-time job to attend college, the amount of work required to be a student leader means it will be impossible for many students.

P.E.

I feel like UVA is trying to be an engaged college. I see that they're changing. That's good, but everything is still very individually focused. I notice if you want something to change, it's on you. I know that's the "UVA way." You have to be democratic and self-governing and whatever. But I feel that UVA should recognize when the university is doing something wrong and take action themselves. They shouldn't wait for students to be like, "Hey, you know the graves next to Gooch Dillard, you should probably fix that." They don't ever think for themselves. They wait for the students to do it. I think the students are more engaged than the actual institution of UVA. Jim Ryan and the Board of Visitors are focused on UVA being a number one public school. "I'll wait for you guys to figure out all the changes we have to do." They have to ask for student input. It's almost as if they don't know what to do. It's like the students are more engaged than the people who are meant to run the place. UVA should know when something's not up to par.

Again, the Gooch Dillard example. There are the graves. People don't even know they exist. The kids who live in Gooch Dillard had to sign this petition to make it known to students that there's a whole graveyard in the backyard. UVA should know there are dead bodies under the ground. I would think that UVA would know to put up a plaque. I know that UVA has this little thing in the ground, but it's not something you would see every day or notice. They have to wait for the students to call them out on everything. I feel like nothing will happen unless students call UVA out. You would think that they'd take responsibility.

The students have to rally everyone together. If it's five kids telling the administration to change something, they're not going to change it. But if you have student signatures from all McIntire, the E-School, Arts and Sciences, if you get hundreds and hundreds and hundreds and thousands of signatures, then I think they will see it is as real a concern. Then they'll change it. I've known some people who put out letters to the administration but do not get enough signatures, so it doesn't get passed on to Jim Ryan. It has to be a concern that can rally a lot of students together or else it won't go to Ryan. I just don't think the administration will give it the necessary attention.

Javaria Abbasi
Class of 2020
College of Arts and Sciences

I think that the Muslim community at UVA is very engaged. I think that the ideals of student governance, however, can sometimes be taken too far. They can become an excuse for faculty to not give support to certain student organizations, to just write an issue off as about student governance. And I definitely think there's a problem where this writing off is disproportionately towards minority CIOs. The university will use the student governance card more with minority CIOs than with certain other CIOs and organizations.

I think it's really hard to improve quality of life for one minority group without working with other minority groups. And sometimes I find in my interactions with certain students that their attitudes towards sexual minorities or certain identities can hurt coalition building. That's just something that worries me. I think part of working together isn't saying that you condone or agree with every aspect of the person's life. There's a common goal that you can work towards. I think sometimes certain moral prerogatives, however, create an unwillingness to work together. And this is true not just of the Muslim community, but also when I've interacted with the Catholic community. I think this has led to problems. The Minority Rights Coalition has done a good job of overcoming these divisions, building coalitions. Attiya Latif, the founder of the Minority Rights Coalition, did a lot of work to bring people together.

Still, I do worry. A lot of our leaders right now are in their fourth years. When they graduate, I worry about that leadership vacuum being filled. For example, Attiya Latif, a hijabi Muslim who is a Jefferson scholar, is now finishing her two Master's degrees—one at Oxford University and the other, I think, at Edinburgh University. I think so many professors and people got to know the Muslim community through her. She became a huge symbol of our community and our presence on-Grounds. Since she's gone, I've seen a pretty marked difference on what non-Muslims know about our community, about what Muslim students care about or are doing. I think she did a good job of bridging the gap and working with departments whereas I think this year, we have had a much more insular focus. That's something I worry about.

K.S.

I absolutely don't think student self-governance should be limited. I think the more power you can give to students, the better. That being said, giving power to the students should not mean that the administration should take blame or responsibility off of themselves. Having a Student Council that deals with a bunch of student issues does not absolve the university in any way. If anything, the administration should become *more* aware of the changes they need to make. Students trying to affect change in the university is a healthy thing for both the students and the university to grow and learn. There are limits on what can be done and by whom, however. There are some administrative restrictions already on becoming a CIO. If it's too similar to another CIO, your group won't be approved. If you've already established your group, you're on a really good path to gaining influence. In terms of the Student Council of each class, especially when you're a first year, that can sometimes be like a popularity contest. You just go with whoever you like, who appeals to you more, or whoever you might have actually heard from during the campaign. If one person lives in Gooch, you're probably going to vote for them because you live in Gooch, that kind of thing. They try to focus on diversity, but I'm pretty sure the Student Council has had a diversity council for a long time. They've tried to do things on diversity, but what can you really do when people aren't too invested in it after they take office, you know? At least, that was an issue we noticed when we got here. I think that there needs to be a better way to spread information and try to get people's platforms known before the election. I vote, but I'm not really too involved with the Student Council. I think that there needs to be a better way for people to understand what candidates are trying to do to be able to decide how to vote.

K.G.

I think this university is engaged when it wants to be and disengaged when it wants to be. I think a lot of the students might feel a particular disconnect between them and the administration or the university as a whole. Specifically, minority students — I think their experience will be very different from a white student here. A white student might tell you, "No, the university is engaged." This is because it's addressing all of their needs because their needs are shared by the majority of the school. But in terms of being engaged and aware of what minority students want and need, I think there's a very clear disengagement.

On the surface, it seems like a negative. But I think it can also be viewed as a positive. That leaves the ball in the court of the students. The students know what they need. They are aware. They can push and actively make an effort to draw these issues to the administration's attention. That's not to say that it's easy. That's not to say that the administration might even be receptive. But it gives students control of their own narrative. It's better that the students who are living that experience every single day on-Grounds bring those issues to light versus an administration that is not necessarily engaged with the minority experience. That is an opportunity. I see a very active effort from minority students to shine a spotlight on their needs, then hold the university accountable when it fails to address these needs.

Y.H.

UVA is always engaged. But when the university tries to bring people into the community, it doesn't always work out. At the same time, you can't force people to do things. I think, to the best of my knowledge and to the best of my ability, I try to be inclusive, and I feel UVA has done about as much as possible. There are a lot of students that just want to do academics. They want to just study and stay in their room, which is totally okay. Totally fine. There are a lot of students that just want to do extracurricular activities. They want to join a bunch of clubs. That's totally fine. So, when it comes to UVA engaging people, I think it's doing a pretty good job, especially President Ryan. He does really well, especially engaging with the community.

"WHY DO STUDENTS HAVE TO GO OUT OF THEIR WAY TO PUSH ADMINISTRATORS TO GET THINGS DONE?"

Al Ahmed
Class of 2020
The School of Education and Human Development

Al Ahmed's narrative initiates a consideration of the value of building more Mus-lim-dominant spaces. He also discusses his mere presence in some leadership roles, such as a Resident Advisor, allows people who are unaware of Islamic principles or who have mistaken beliefs to learn and then change their perspectives. Drawing from similar experiences, Muslim students at UVA then expand this discussion of the difficult (but necessary) work of educating others about Islam.

When I first came to UVA, I was in culture-shock. I went to a majority-minority high school. When I came here, Grounds was very visibly white. So it was amazing to see that the Muslim Students Association (MSA) was large and vibrant. It was reassuring to see a large number of people like me, that I could relate to. who understand, and who are going through similar struggles, If I didn't have that space, honestly, my experience would definitely have been very different and tough. The college environment is very difficult when you're trying to be a practicing Muslim: not drinking, not taking drugs, and not engaging in related activities. I remember my first year, everything was centered around drinking, going out, and partying. At first, I would make up excuses to avoid those things. I just felt a little out of place and disheartened that everyone around me was doing it, but I wasn't. Eventually, I gained the confidence to tell my hallmates, "I don't drink, smoke, or engage in those kinds of activities because I'm a practicing Muslim." They were actually very respectful and accepting.

Since then, I've been proud of my identity by being as vocally and visibly Muslim as I can. I try to engage with people about Islam whether it be in different groups, organizations, or classes. I try to engage with others because, honestly, people are just uninformed about Islam. They see what's constantly in the media and, whether they realize it or not, it implicitly impacts them. Most people don't really have a relationship with Muslims or with Islam. It's hard to blame them for holding or believing certain stereotypes, especially if they have no interaction with Muslims. Hopefully, with me just being in the room, I can make a difference. Hypothetically, someone could see something in the media depicting negative stereotypes, but then, maybe, after getting to know me, they're like, "I know Al who's Muslim. There's no way he thinks like that or feels like that." I feel it helps people having examples of Muslims they know that are "just like us" or "just another UVA student," just another "American Muslim."

In the classroom setting, if there's ever any remark, inference, bias, or microaggressions, I never attack the individual. Sometimes, it can get very difficult when you hear ignorant statements being made. It can be very difficult to control your emotions and not lash out. I've taken a few Islam-focused classes. I have been in discussion sections where students have some biases or stereotypes. I try to challenge those statements from a good place, not coming at them with, "Oh, you're wrong. You're an awful person for thinking that way." Instead of attacking the person, I challenge the ideas and thoughts: "Where is that coming from? Can you support that? What's making you say these things?"

I remember somebody said, "Oh, but women are so oppressed in Islam." Then that person gave examples from Islamic countries and certain incidents. I responded, "Sure, it's possible that potentially in some countries, women are oppressed. People aren't perfect. But if you look at the religion, you look at the prime example of what Islam should be. You can look at the Prophet Muhammad's (PBUH) example of his own wife, Khadijah. The Prophet's wife was a successful and renowned businesswoman. Remember Islam came to a society and time where people were burying their daughters alive out of shame. Women were treated as less than human and were given little to no rights. Islam established equity, gave women rights and liberated them over 1400 years ago when movements like the Women's suffrage movement just happened in 1920. The fourth chapter of the Quran is dedicated to women and establishes these rights. Furthermore, there are numerous examples throughout history where Islam has empowered women, including key figures like Fatima al-Fihri, who was the first person known to found a university. People see the countries oppressing women or practicing Islam in a way that misconstrues its true teachings to fulfill their political agendas closing. I feel challenging and countering such statements and sentiments is important because rarely do people know or see the full picture and context.

I have had professors who made controversial remarks with regard to Islam, saying things against the true teachings of the religion. Teachers who impose their personal beliefs into the classroom rather than teaching neutrally and as unbiased as possible. It is almost as if they have a personal vendetta with the religion. I know I am not alone when I say this type of belief. I have heard similar grievances from other Muslim students. Just to give an example, I remember a class where we were discussing the story of Isra and Mi'raj, which is the sacred journey the Prophet Muhammad (PBUH) took in the Islamic tradition. By the way the professor was talking about it, they made the story seem like a fairy tale. It was clear they thought there was no legitimacy to the account. That is what the professor was trying to get across. I guess if you're looking at it from an outside perspective, it can be seen that way. However, if you're a Muslim student, you see it as an attack on your faith. That's not the professor's job. They are there to teach and present the material. Students should be able to draw their own conclusions from it. If they do offer their opinions, that's fine, but they should also offer counter opinions. The professor shouldn't be questioning teachings of any faith or trying to prove a religion has flaws or is wrong. The job of a professor should be just to present and teach the material in an unbiased manner. But from this professor, I felt, more often than not, he was imposing his views and presented a biased and overall wrong narrative of Islam unfortunately.

However, I also had a positive experience with another professor who has a very strong background, education, and is well accomplished. In this class, the professor did a good job of presenting Islam in a fair way. As a result, the class engaged in many meaningful dialogues and the discussions were very lively. Overall, I've been lucky to have mostly positive classroom experiences when it comes to Islam classes. But I do believe if you compare UVA to other universities and institutions, I do feel like we're lacking and could make improvements to have a stronger Islamic Studies department. Particularly, I personally believe professors who teach Islam should have a strong Islamic background and are scholars in Islamic law, theology, and jurisprudence.

When it comes to the political climate on campus, like election time, or when there's polarizing incidents that happen on campus, I wish that UVA faculty could just be at the forefront more, just being there for students, being supportive of them, and listening to our needs and our demands. There is an election in 2020, right? We know things are probably going to happen. There were incidents that happened leading up to and after the last presidential election in 2016. There were Islamophobic flyer-ing and chalking incidents, Muslim students getting harassed, and their dorms getting vandalized. There were a lot of incidents. It was really unfortunate. I wish there was a way for administrators, faculty, and those in positions of power to be on top of such incidents and take direct action in response. If there were precautions in place and a game plan on how to identify and hold the perpetrators of Islamophobic incidents accountable, I feel like a lot of students would really appreciate these efforts.

I remember once when there was a proposal that resulted from a joint effort by multiple minority organizations. A student accessed the public document of the proposal and vandalized it by writing a bunch of racial slurs including writing something against the MSA. To my knowledge they never found out who did it. I believe there was an official investigation into the matter. Again, though, there was unfortunately nothing much done about it. It's very difficult to prevent things like this from happening. If anybody wants to do something like that, they can do it. Unfortunately, that's just how it is. This is where accountability is so important. If someone believes they can get away with it, they are more likely to continue doing things like that. Incidents like this show that when incidents happen to minority students, which includes Muslim students, there isn't strong action or much follow up. I can't say this is the case for sure, but I can only imagine if something similar happened to a white student or to a group of white individuals, how would the administration react? My hope is that the response would be equal regardless of the student or organization attacked.

Why do students have to go out of their way to push administrators to get things done? For example, the prayer space. To just get a larger prayer space, I want to say we have had to push for at least three years. Now, finally, there was an official proposal put together led by the Virginia Interfaith Coalition and Muslim Students Association. An interfaith prayer room will finally be established. But again, just looking behind the effort and the push, the discussions that have been happening for such a long time, and now, finally, they're doing it. Why did it take so long? At least now there will finally be a prayer space. It will be of benefit to many students. It also shows the importance of continuous advocacy, that they are listening and making an effort to accommodate our needs. However, there is always more that can be done.

As I think about my time at UVA, I think the most meaningful work I've done is to make our community feel that there is a safe space for them at UVA. I've continuously tried to do things for our community even in dark and challenging times, such as when these Islamophobic incidents happen. My goal is to help Muslims at UVA feel united as a community and to be there supporting each other irrespective of our differences. I've always thought about the community and am always thinking about areas where I can help make a difference. I try my best to help improve things, help Muslim students with their needs, and I trying to be a voice for all Muslim students at UVA. That's been my experience. I've done that every year in whatever ways I can. For me, advocating for my communities and finding ways to better the university defines my UVA experience.

During my term as President of MSA, my goals were to reach out, work with, and build a relationship with administrators and other student organizations. For example, last year, Ramadan fell during the final exams. We asked university administration to ensure a statement went out to professors to ensure accommodations would be made for Muslim students who would be were fasting all day. Additionally, we worked with dining services to have accommodations for the pre-dawn suhoor meal and to have dining options open later for breaking the fast during iftar. As a Student Council Representative, whenever incidents happened affecting the Muslim community, I would try to make sure the Council was aware and that they would sign onto or create legislation demonstrating their support of Muslim students. For instance, when the shootings of the mosque during the Friday prayer happened in Christchurch, New Zealand, I worked to make sure Student Council expressed their support. Additionally, the MSA organized a vigil and worked to have other organizations involved because we are stronger as a community when we support each other. I also tried to empower and challenge Muslims to get involved in the UVA community. One way I did this was through Housing and Residence Life by recruiting Muslim students to become RA's. When I first started, there were very few Muslim students. Now there are a lot of Muslim students that are serving as RA's and making an impact on the lives of first year residents. I made a similar effort with Student Council. There are now several Muslim Student Council Representatives and members. I'm just really trying to challenge, encourage, and push Muslim students, especially younger Muslim underclassmen students, to get involved in whatever meaningful ways they can and leave their mark on UVA.

I was also one of the founding members of The Muslim Institute for Leadership and Empowerment (MILE). The goal of MILE was to create a space for young Muslim students to engage and learn soft skills that other leadership programs are providing but Muslim students aren't getting offered, such as public speaking, interviewing, resume development, career building, etc. We also wanted to create an alternative space where Muslim students could engage in challenging and meaningful dialogue, explore Muslim identity and intersectionality, and what it means to be a Muslim leader. The establishment of MILE is an example of where having relationships with university administration is crucial and important. With the help of a friend, we brought forward the proposal for MILE to a Dean and offered their support to make it a reality. The rest was history.

In empowering Muslim students and encouraging them to pursue positions of leadership, one of the hardest obstacles is rejection. Given the competitive nature at UVA, that's one of the hardest obstacles. I always tell them not to be discouraged by rejection. I know I've encouraged a good number of students who tried out for different things—Honor, UJC, Student Council, University Guide Service, Orientation Life, Resident Advisor, etc. Some of them were accepted, which is great, right? But others, unfortunately, weren't. I try to support them through rejections, being vulnerable with them and letting them know of the many things and positions that I didn't get. It can be defeating at first, but we should not let it define who we are. Failure is part of the process. No matter what opportunity is available or comes our way, we should do our best within our capacity and then live with the results. As long as we put our best foot forward, we can't control what happens afterwards. I am proud of how far the Muslim community at UVA has come, and I am excited to see what the future holds. It has been an honor and pleasure to have been a part of the Muslim community in Charlottesville. I hope to continue to be a voice for Muslims wherever my path takes me.

Hisham Ahmad
Class of 2021
College of Arts and Sciences

I really like the diversity, or, at least, I like the diversity that UVA is trying to achieve. I like how UVA has so many CIOs, so many clubs and organizations that represent different cultures, religions, and backgrounds. The student population overall, though? Well, I think everyone knows that there's clearly more of a certain group of people at UVA than others. Definitely minority groups are not as represented at UVA as much as at other universities. I still really appreciate that UVA is trying to achieve that diversity with the new classes and new generations. Still, there were definitely certain situations where I felt uncomfortable being part of a minority group.

For instance, sometimes I have to pray in a class because I'm in a hurry and I don't want to miss my prayer, since I then have to go to another class. I get that there's the "mindfulness room" for prayer, but, first of all, it's a small space. Second, it's only in one area of Grounds, which is Newcomb. If you're on the other side of Grounds and you need to pray somewhere, it's hard for you. If you find that spot, if someone walks in on you, you just feel so uncomfortable and awkward. They also give you looks of, "What are you doing?" which feels very unwelcoming. At those moments, I feel like the community is also not educated enough about different religions and different groups. I feel like it would also be a nice thing to have some sort of understanding of different religions, cultures, and ideologies.

I'm also an RA, a resident advisor. Walking into that first meeting with my residents, all of whom are all from the same race, I was uncomfortable being the only minority. Just walking between them, I felt so uncomfortable. I felt that lack of diversity, which I did not appreciate beforehand. I was hoping at least my hall would be more diverse and have people from different backgrounds. It got weird when we had an activity called "I.D. Cards," where we basically had to identify ourselves. Most of them had that same exact ID: They all had that white race, higher middle class, Christians, coming from a rich area in Virginia, or, if out of state, still from a rich area. Then it came to me. It was more like, "Oh! I'm from the Middle East. I'm Arab. I'm Muslim. Middle class." So you see it; you see that gap. It's pretty obvious. Still, I was able to overcome some of those feelings through being in different spaces at the UVA, such as the Multicultural Center or different CIOs.

Where I came from, Jordan, I didn't find that it was a big thing to talk about racism or discrimination. The United States is a melting pot. We have so many different groups, so many different races and people from different backgrounds and ideologies. But living in the Middle East, in Jordan, we didn't have that big of a problem. Being here was kind of different for me. It was new for me to see how certain groups are under-represented and how certain groups have a history of unequal rights.

Regardless of all those moments, there are also great things about UVA. I feel like we should also focus on the similarities and the good things about UVA. Recently what's happening is that people are trying to focus more and more on our differences, more and more on how UVA is not a welcoming inclusive community for us to live in. I feel there should be more of a push for each one of us to be proud and happy that we're at a really good university. Our university is known in the nation and known worldwide. When I found out that some of my friends in Jordan as well as some of my friends in Arab countries knew about UVA, I was surprised. Honestly, I thought that one of them was lying to me that they knew UVA. I was like, "Okay, you're pretending you know it, but you don't." But they actually did. It makes me proud. It makes me proud that UVA has its place and is trying to put itself on the world map.

K.S.

I know someone who used to go to a really, really small college. She was one of the only Muslims there. She didn't have Muslims in her classes, and she was struggling to get an MSA going. She went to Virginia Tech's MSA all the time because her college is so small. At UVA, because we have a Muslim presence here, we're able to do those things whereas if it was one Muslim person in all of the university, the university might not hear as much as a Muslim would want to be heard. I think that our presence here has a lot of weight in that we're able to actually ask for a prayer room. We're able to actually hold Jummah on-Grounds. I think if a school is similar to UVA, then students will have a similar experience. But I think that it's not every single school where Muslims have this experience.

We do have a strong Honor Code, which most people try to go by. We do have "fostering a community of trust" and those kinds of things. President Jim Ryan has his outline of really flowery, but nice, kinds of goals that he wants to achieve. Diversity is one of them. I feel like the culture at UVA is positive for Muslim Americans and that it's not necessarily so at other universities in Virginia. I think the UVA MSA here could do more to be inclusive and to get people in the MSA that are not necessarily Muslim. No CIO is going to limit membership, like, "Oh, you can't come because you're Muslim." I have friends who are in this Christian Fellowship CIO. I hang out with them all the time. I go to their events because they're good people. So no CIO is going to limit, or at least they're not allowed to, exclude people because of their identity. I think UVA's MSA could do more in terms of just trying to get our events out there. Not making it like, "Oh, this is a free food event, come! But more like, "This is a chance for you to mingle with people who might not have the same background as you. And that's so interesting. So come."

CHAPTER THREE
Community

Saajid Hasan, Hira Azher, A.N., Omer Gorashi, Fadumo Hussein, Saqib Rizvi, M.M., Sumaya Mohammed

Community is a tricky term. It is often understood through nostalgic frameworks. Harmonious neighborhoods, sports leagues, and state fairs often dominate. Actual communities, however, are spaces of negotiation, planning, and labor. It is this definition of community that the students in this chapter invoke when discussing the Muslim student community at UVA. What they detail is the means by which individual experiences of being under-represented in university governance and organizations are addressed by collective action. And in the process, they demonstrate how a community can work together to enable a flourishing of multiple identities, traditions, and practices. In doing so, the students do not gloss over tensions and division still to be resolved. Nor do these students represent the process of expanding the definition of a "Muslim" student as easy, simple. It is not the dream, but the labor of building community that is showcased. And in this way, the student voices which begin this chapter noting how UVA's institutions do not adequately "recognize" or address the needs of Muslim students, also demonstrate the process by which the Grounds can support a more fertile and enriched environment.

"I THINK MUSLIMS HAVE AMAZING POTENTIAL AND CAPACITY"

Saajid Hasan
Class of 2019
College of Arts and Sciences
Class of 2020
Frank Batten School of Leadership and Public Policy

Saajid Hasan initiates a conversation on the experience of being a "minority within a minority." Hasan highlights the diversity that exists within the Muslim community which, from the outside looking in, or even from looking within, seems to be unrecognized. In doing so, he discusses how this lack of recognition of multi-layered minority identities causes frustrations with the UVA Muslim Student Association and Council.

There's an interesting dynamic where, given Muslims are a minority and marginalized group, there's this tendency for members outside of this group, such as just the general UVA administration or community, to view Muslims as one single monolithic group rather than a diverse community in and of itself. There's this tendency to just view all Muslims as one. With that in mind, I think the administration has done an effective job generally for what it knows. It's mostly up to the Muslim Student Association (MSA) and MSA Council to acknowledge and/or address issues of diversity within the Muslim community.

There are different layers to being Muslim. For instance, I am not just a Muslim student; I'm also very interested in public policy, politics, and economics, and I have other interests as well. I think it's not necessarily being Muslim that drives my opinions and beliefs towards everything because, even though we follow one religion, we are multilayered people. There was this TED Talk that I remember watching one time and it discusses how, as minorities, we shouldn't fall into this myth of the single story. As in, as Muslims, we can't just imagine that our whole life revolves around, I guess, being Muslim, and that that one identity informs every single thing that we do and are interested in. There are other parts of our identity. I'm also from Northern Virginia, my family is from Hyderabad, India; these are also very many parts of my identity that influence my views.

As Muslims growing up in the West, we have to learn how to deal with balancing our different identities. Being a diaspora child, it feels like you have two homes all the time or you have two different personalities you need to portray depending on the situation. I guess it makes it difficult to find out who you really are, so it makes that conversation a little bit more complicated. At the end of the day though, you will find that union between your culture, religion, and Western identity. I think that balance will come. I think college plays a really important role in helping you figure out that balance. External pressure definitely makes this conversation and struggle within yourself difficult because these are very internal experiences. How religious you are is a very internal, spiritual thing. It comes from your heart. How much you feel in tune with your mother-heritage or culture, again, is a very internal experience.

Therefore, when you have people expecting certain things out of you, then that really just distorts that whole journey within yourself, and so that makes it very difficult. Discussing the Muslim narrative in academic spaces, again, reinforces this notion that there's only one Muslim narrative. And that's been, personally, a struggle for me because I was raised and am a Shia Muslim. Whenever we discuss issues of Islam, it's almost always typically from the majority Sunni perspective. There's nothing wrong with speaking from that perspective, but it just adds to this willingness or desire to put all Muslims in one box and label them all as a marginalized community, which is true, but it also ignores the diversity within traditions and impedes meaningful discussion on how to bridge the Muslim community together. Because, for marginalized communities to really be uplifted and empower themselves, there needs to be some soul searching done within that community itself, and in this case, within the Muslim community, and understanding its own struggles and issues and how to overcome them together.

I'm very vocally Muslim in most places that I go to, but it depends on where. Say if I'm in a majority white space, as in most of my classes, then I don't jump to saying, "I'm Shia" because it's not going to be that relevant to them, so people just know that I'm a Muslim, not necessarily of which specific tradition. Especially in Batten—Batten's a very white space. Our current MSA president (2019-2020) is one of the only other people, I think, in Batten that is Muslim. I can't think of anyone else in the MSA that's even doing the master's in public policy (MPP) program. Therefore, in a space like that where it's majority non-Muslim, then I'll just shift to a general Muslim identity, but when it comes to Muslim spaces, when it's relevant for a conversation, then I'm fairly open about my further identity, which is a Shia.

Having to represent your identity in every single context you find your-self is very tiring. It's very burdensome as a minority. Even within a Muslim space, I feel as if I have to represent Shias, which is just another burden. So it feels like it's a double burden on me. When it comes to the Batten space, it's public policy and government, so it's a very white field. There was actually a class activity that we were doing just a few days ago. There was an issue of Islam that came up in the case study we were studying, and a member of the military in our course opened up the conversation with something blatantly Islamophobic. Everyone was looking around the class, and I was stunned, thinking, "Really?! Literally, no one's going to say anything?" I just felt like I had to say something right away to set it straight, and I did. This need and obligation to do things like this, after a while, makes one feel very vulnerable and exhausted. And then on the other hand, when you're a minority within a minority, it's doubly exhausting.

In the MSA, for instance, for me, it really comes down to the MSA Council. It's less about individual members of the MSA because I feel that there's a general lack of awareness that non-minority Muslims experience growing up towards understanding other traditions within Islam. Therefore, the issue comes with the MSA Council and what seems like their unwilling-ness or discomfort with acknowledging diversity within Muslim traditions. So ultimately, if Council were to take the lead and champion these conver-sations, that would really have a ripple effect when it comes to just campus culture in general, and then even affect as we go into classes as well and have more frank discussions. This past semester was actually quite frustrating be-cause there was an issue with asking the MSA Council to acknowledge the commemoration of the martyrdom of Imam Hussain, a revered figure in the Shia Muslim tradition, which is a very serious mourning time, primarily for Shia Muslims, but it is also commemorated by other Muslims. When trying to get Council to just send out a simple broadcast message, they were very reluctant and cited what felt like unreasonable concerns. They just found cre-ative ways to refuse to do certain things under the guise of preserving unity, but what ends up happening is just a systematic erasure of minority traditions within the MSA. And when they do issue statements, what would end up happening, in effect, is they would issue a certain statement but wash it out of any distinguishing features that would cater to a minority tradition and instead try to make it as general as possible.

I have thought about running for the MSA Council, but what turns me off is the idea that I would just be put into a box: "He's just that Shia guy running and that's all he's going to talk about." Honestly, that is not really what I want to be doing because I have other aspects of myself, but what it comes down to is just the tokenizing minority. That tokenization occurs as a Muslim in a white space, and then as a Shia Muslim in a Muslim space, too, so it's a double burden. That's what I feel would happen if I ran for Council, that I would end up getting boxed into that label. It wouldn't really be the best way to advocate for what I believe. That's why my goal with the Council lately has been to push them from the outside and mobilize all the other Shias that I know in the Charlottesville community and at UVA. We did that successfully about a month ago when we all showed up to a Council meeting and forced this conversation to happen. I felt the need to bring pressure from outside because it seemed like they were not ready to have that conversation genuinely from inside the space.

The support of the new chaplain has been one positive development. I think having her as just a support for all students and a way to voice some of our concerns has been really impactful. Therefore, having long-standing support would be beneficial. It's also important for future Council members and future members of the MSA to always be aware of these issues within the Muslim community and recognize that it's not a weakness at all. It speaks to the richness of the Muslim faith that there can be different interpretations and debates about what Islam means. This speaks to the richness of the faith and how there's so much that Muslims can learn from each other. Furthermore, projecting this to the outside, such conversations with the non-Muslim community would also make the Muslim community look stronger and more empowered to succeed in the future as well. There's an internal and external dynamic in play.

The MSA Council has the capacity to do so much. We have really talented and committed people within the Council and within the general MSA. Consider all the pre-med students, all the high achieving students—our parents have definitely instilled a great work ethic in all of us. I think that speaks to the success of the Muslim community in this country on an objective measure. So I think Muslims have amazing potential and capacity to achieve so much. It's just about making, I guess, the right decisions and having more inclusion, different voices, and not trying to stifle dissent within the community.

For example, being a part of the Muslim Institute for Leadership and Empowerment (MILE) was case in point. With MILE, some motivated Muslims got together, Al and Zakir, and said, "We want to start a whole initiative for Muslim students." They applied to the Multicultural Student Services, Office of the Dean of Students, these university arms, and created this whole program from scratch. It was such a privilege to be a part of that first cohort in that program in 2019. I think that really reflects how much UVA students, and more specifically Muslim UVA students in this case, care and then also how much the UVA administration also cares. MILE, for me, was a really great experience. It being separate from the MSA, I felt like I had more of a space there that the MSA couldn't provide for minority Muslims in particular. MILE presented a space outside of MSA where we could have more pointed conversations as we definitely did in some of the sessions, and it was really important. I believe MILE is going to continue to grow in importance within the university Muslim space in the coming years, and I hope it will, Insha'Allah.

When it comes to a policy prescription for the administration, the administration can't change people's views and just be a public lecturer for issues of Islam or other marginalized communities for the whole public. You can't just give a lecture in John Paul Jones Arena to all of the university students and say, "This is how you should act." It's not practical. So I think it really just comes down to Muslims themselves having greater mobilization and capacity to advocate for themselves. That's definitely a burden like I've already mentioned, and that's going to be a challenge moving forward.

Diversity within the Muslim community is something that MSA Council is very scared of acknowledging, but then everyone's always asking for diversity in other spaces, so this is a double standard. The issue is not at all with individual Muslims. It's more of a structural thing. That's something that is left to be decided by communities themselves, organizations, not really the university administration. It's not the university's responsibility. This might seem counterintuitive, but there's so many different complexities of minorities, communities, and just identities. As such, it's just not practical for the university to find out ways to cater to every individual need. Therefore, that's what I think is so powerful about student self-governance. It is definitely a burden on communities but for the right reason: local communities or local organizations, like [the] MSA, are the ones in the best position to figure out the needs of their own community. Ultimately, the university administration has to concern itself with making the school the best academic space for students to continue coming here for years. I think that really just has to be the priority of the university, and a lot of power has to be left to student organizations. I think the university definitely does that sufficiently, with funding

MILE for example. That's a step in the right direction. The rest of the work ultimately has to just be within communities because I wouldn't expect Dean Groves to know everything about our community. Ultimately, the university is busy being a great public university.

This trend towards secularism in universities is not going away. There's really nothing that can be done to stop something like that, and I'm not saying that that is an issue. When thinking about how such secular places can support Muslim students like ourselves, however, it's primarily about making sure there will always be a space for Muslims coming into the university to express themselves freely. And that's where the goal of the MSA comes in. It's meant to be a space for Muslim students to come in, but of course that also is not without its own challenges, as I've discussed so far. Those internal challenges in turn, however, really just speak to the complexity of the Muslim experience in general at universities and outside of university. The Muslim story is not one monolithic narrative at all. It's easy to present itself that way for the purposes of a political agenda, but it's so much more complex than that, and it's not something that can just be addressed by a single policy, either.

Quick disclaimer to the MSA and Muslim community in general: there's no beef or anything that I have. This isn't creating divisions within the Muslim community. It's more about demanding that these narratives be included within conversations and that other eyes are not excluded because it's on the MSA to make a space.

"WE TRIED TO RE-IMAGINE A SPACE FOR MUSLIM STUDENTS THAT PRIORITIZES THE EXPERIENCE OF MARGINALIZED MUSLIMS"

Hira Azher
Class of 2021
College of Arts and Sciences

Hira Azher's narrative initiates a consideration of the experience of being a Muslim student representative at UVA as well as what it could (and should) mean to hold such a position of power. In the process, Azher speaks about the establishment and goals of Muslims United at UVA. As such, her narrative discusses the persistent effort required by students to create safe spaces for minorities that too often feel a lack of belonging even in spaces meant for them.

The atmosphere of UVA depends on which classrooms and which spaces you're in. UVA is a predominantly white school, and that is reflected in all of its classrooms. Oftentimes, even courses focusing on Islam or on cultural studies that aren't white, those classes are still dominated and sometimes even taught by white professors who don't necessarily know or understand Islam or the different cultures outside of an academic context. And that reality is something that's irremovable from being a student at UVA, at a predominantly white school. All of these conversations and all of the spaces that you're in, well, are very hard to separate from whiteness. To clarify, what I mean by *whiteness* is not just somebody's physical appearance but all of the power that comes with whiteness, the privilege, the ability to overpower conversations, and the ability to act in ways that are systemically and historically violent, including Islamophobic, racist, misogynistic, and all those other things.

Regarding my experiences with Islam, more specifically, I've experienced a lot of different things from UVA in general and Muslim spaces in particular. With the general UVA, I think a lot of people's understandings of Islam, especially white students at UVA, are flawed or uninformed. As much as we would like to think that they would have been exposed to and thus more knowledgeable about certain things, they're not—at least not in my experience. Since we have these ideas of elite cosmopolitan-ish types of institutions, we think that people there are well-versed, well-traveled, and have exposure when the reality couldn't be further from that thought. It is still very common to hear superficial and uninterrogated thoughts about Islam, especially about Muslim women, their choice to wear hijab, whether they even have one or not–which by the way, they absolutely do—and even hearing them talk about "the Muslim world" as this one thing/place that exists where everybody is homogenous within. Therefore, just hearing the ways people would reference Islam, reference being a Muslim, and the microaggressions that result from it, it is very clear that they have little to no understanding of what Islam actually is.

Last year in my anthropology class, it was kind of a capstone course where we were all writing our anthropology theses, about 10-to-20-page papers, there was this one student. He was a white guy and was writing a paper about arranged marriages in what he quoted to be "the Muslim world." From the very beginning, when we were all sharing our proposals with the class and I heard his, I was a little like, "Okay, that's weird!" But at the moment, I did not feel like I had the right words to articulate how it was weird and how it made me–or would make anyone of a similar background—quite uncomfortable. Plus, it is not like I could control what project he does anyway, so I just let it go. Soon after, however, when we were doing peer reviews, I received his paper. As I was reading it, sure enough, my prior uneasiness was substantiated. First of all, all of his sources were taken from white authors in this colonial/post-colonial era, around the mid-1900s, and they were often British. Second, the only pool he was pulling from was Saudi Arabia, which is what he was defining as "the Muslim world" and portraying the experiences of Saudi women as the representative experience of all Muslim women. What's more, he didn't use a single account from an actual Muslim woman living in Saudi Arabia; all he used were anthropological pieces or post-colonial pieces written by white men or British colonists, describing what was happening and what they were seeing in Saudi Arabia. Consequently, he wrote this whole paper trying to describe what arranged marriage is in "the Muslim world", which, according to him, was just Saudi Arabia, without using any accounts of Muslim women, and was talking about how it was a patriarchal process. He also, in a deluded attempt at fairness, said something along the lines of, "Even in the West, the society is patriarchal." I guess I can see why he would make that comparison, but it didn't remove the fact that his paper, as a whole, was clearly embedded with ignorance, Islamophobia, and misogyny towards specifically Muslim women: assuming that they were oppressed, assuming they had no voice, and, more importantly, not using their voice in the piece that he was writing.

And so I left all that feedback on his peer review, hoping that he would take my suggestions, you know, an actual Muslim woman, and make some changes. When we were presenting our projects on the final day, however, sadly but unsurprisingly, it seemed like he didn't change anything or take any of my recommendations. Even though, in the peer review, I explicitly said, "To me, as a Muslim woman, it is really scary and problematic that you are writing all this but not taking any of the experiences of actual Muslim women into account," he didn't change anything in his presentation. As soon as he finished presenting, I remember, I took the entire time of Q&A - it's about 10 minutes for every presentation - to call out all the issues I was seeing. I think the rest of the class was taken aback when I did that because up until that point, nobody had really taken the question time seriously; it was just like one of those formalities. This time, however, I was so frustrated because he was not understanding any of my feedback, so I voiced my concerns. He was just taking it as if I was attacking him though, which, to a degree, I was but only because he seemed heedless of the dire consequences to me and others like me that would result from what he is presenting to be intellectual work. He was propagating these lies and misconceptions that are so dangerous to Muslim women and violent structurally. Even now, just thinking about it, I'm getting so mad. And that experience is the first thing that comes to mind when asked about the experience of Islam in a classroom at a PWI.

In terms of representation of Muslims within UVA, it is tricky because it's easy to fall into identity politics, like, "Where do we see Muslims represented?" Although it is important, I think identity politics also has its limits because for a lot of us who see UVA as an institution of violence, harm, and oppression, to see Muslims represented in that institution, there is still this thought in the back of our head, like, "Yes, it's great that we see people who look like ourselves, but do we idolize them when we know that they're also contributing to these power dynamics?" Therefore, although it is great to see representation, we have to ask, at what cost? Are they contributing to this institution and to this harm towards other students at UVA, whether it be Black students, low-income students, and all the legacies of UVA of genocide of Native Americans, of slavery, and all of these legacies that have really never had any sort of justice, reparations, or healing?

When I first started at UVA, it was very meaningful to me to see Muslims in these space, but as I've grown to learn more about the university and grown in my own politics, it's become a little disappointing. To see Muslims in positions of power, in ways that make them complicit instead of using that power to help their communities, whether it be Muslim communities or even other communities that are marginalized, is very disappointing. Having a Muslim on the board of visitors, or a Muslim working for President Ryan, to me, is not something exciting or something to be proud of now, but even a little embarrassing because we as Muslims could have used this collective power that we have to fight against these institutions that are causing harm to us, and our neighbors, and our brothers and sisters. Especially, when our religion and our Prophet Mohammed (PBUH) himself has told us to advocate for justice saying, "If you see an injustice, try to stop it with your hand. And if you can't stop it with your hand, stop it with your tongue. And if you can't stop it with your tongue, at least know in your heart that it's unjust." And even when we learn about Imam Ali of the Shia tradition and how he tirelessly fought for justice, we know that fighting for what is right is a core part of Islam. Therefore, it becomes difficult for me to see Muslims represented in these institutions of UVA in ways that feel unjust, maybe not to our community, but to other communities and other marginalized folks.

To some extent, I do understand why they are or perhaps feel like they need to be complicit, because as long as you're not a white man in this country, you are, to a degree, forced into taking certain positions simply because you are inherently politicized. Being a Muslim in America is inherently political. It reminds me of this quote from my favorite author, Arundhati Roy, "As soon as a breath enters the body, it's political," and I feel that way about anybody. Therefore, as Muslims living in the United States, we're inherently forced into these stances, whether we want to be in them or not. I believe that is unfair to us as well. It usually comes down to survival, too, where we draw the line of us being complicit with this institution versus us just trying to survive in this institution that's not necessarily built for people like us. And everybody draws that line differently! I am reminded of this other quote by Audre Lorde, 'The master's tools will never dismantle the master's house." To that end, we should know that we can't use the tools of this institution to help our communities, but at some point, we also have to survive. It's a master's house, we also have to make a living; we have to, in some ways, even appeal to white people and be digestible to them.

On that note, it's also interesting to notice that, oftentimes, the Muslims represented in these institutional positions are the Muslims that are the most digestible to white people. They're not the radical or what is deemed the radical left Muslims. They're the Muslims who are in the center or the Muslims who don't like to argue. They're the Muslims who are seen sometimes closest in proximity with whiteness: Muslims who are well educated, who speak well, who are able to talk and interact like white folks and fit into those environments. It's always those Muslims that are in those representative positions which is super frustrating because, personally, I would give more slack if the Muslims in these positions are those who are from marginalized identities, in terms of their race, their sexuality, their gender, et cetera. Muslims who might need these positions to get some sort of institutional backing for themselves because they don't have that already. Unsurprisingly, however, it ends up being the Muslims that already have that institutional backing, some privilege, and certain identities or positions that already give them power— whether it be being light skinned, being part white, being a Sunni Muslim, being a cis-het Muslim, et cetera—that end up in those positions.

Which is not to say that there are no such Muslims in any leadership or representational places. For instance, a Muslim is currently the chair of the Minority Rights Coalition. And I think it is so empowering to see Muslims in those kinds of leftist revolutionary spaces, being representatives in these spaces of resistance. Nonetheless, I wish we could see more of that, because again, I understand that, to some degree, there is this kind of pressure to fit these molds of whiteness, these molds that come from colonial-settler-ism, racism, and hetero-patriarchy. At some point, however, especially with Muslims who enjoy certain privileges, myself included by the way, we have a duty to not be complicit because we have the privilege to speak up, to fight against these institutions and face less or no violence in comparison to our Black brothers and sisters or queer brothers and sisters, especially since, like I said before, it is our type of Muslims that are mostly in these institutional position due to said privileges.

In regard to why we don't see more of the marginalized Muslim communities in these positions, I think it comes down back to understanding our relationships with institutions of power. Now, I want to be clear: I don't think marginalized Muslims "should" be taking these positions or that we need more marginalized Muslims in these positions, because at the end of the day, these are oppressive positions to be in. However, to answer the question of why we don't see as many, first of all, these positions require power to attain, and the more marginalized you are, the less access you have to that power and resources: you might not have had the same education as some of the more privileged Muslims; you might not have the same language and ability to articulate to audiences that are white and appeal to them; and you might not dress the same or speak the same languages that they do. Altogether, the more marginalized Muslims tend to be in farther proximity to whiteness, and that inherently results in less power and less ability to attain those positions. Furthermore, I don't want to speak on behalf of all marginalized Muslims and all those different identities, but I think there is also less of a desire to be part of an institution that is oppressing you and your community. And that is something that I have come to realize recently: these institutions will never be for us because they were never *intended* to be for us. From the very start, their very design was made to exclude us. Even if we are in these power positions, these institutions will not be good for our community. They will not lead us to liberation or the justice that we desire. Therefore, knowing that, maybe it is better to put our energies into spaces that will lead us to that liberation, into spaces of resistance, spaces of revolution, and communities of care, instead of trying to reform these institutions that seem irreformable.

That is my experience of Islam with UVA as whole, in terms of my experience with Muslim spaces in particular; it is also complicated. I think, with every school, there is a Muslim Student Association (MSA) which, most of the time, is the main Muslim space. However, similar to what I mentioned earlier about leadership and institutional positions, this organization also tends to be dominated by white or white-passing Arab students and South Asians, including my own identity, like Pakistani, Indian, Bengalis. Again, Muslims with some sort of privilege. As such, my relationship with the MSA at UVA had ups and downs and it was complicated.

To give some context, I was raised in Ames, Iowa, which is a very small place; I think about 90% of the population was white, and it had very few Muslims. Afterward, I moved to Virginia Beach, which, again, doesn't really have a huge Muslim community. Therefore, I never grew up around many Muslims or ever had a close-knit group of Muslim friends. Consequently, when I came to UVA, that close-knit Muslim community was something that I was seeking out internally without even realizing it. I was seeking out this group of people whom, I was told, would have similar experiences, values, and beliefs that I did. I had internalized this notion that Muslim American identity is homogenous, and I will inherently, because I'm a Muslim American, feel the same way as the other Muslim Americans around me. Like I said, because I had never really interacted with so many Muslim communities, I didn't realize the diversity of thought and the diversity of values and beliefs that exist within Muslim communities. Therefore, coming into UVA, I was really excited to meet these Muslim friends whom I had assumed were going to be my BFFs. To this end I was initially very involved in the MSA. The whole welcome week, I was going to all those events, and then the more interactions I had with the MSA, the more I started to see flaws in this perfect idea that I had conjured in my head of what a Muslim community was.

Additionally, I experienced a lot of misogyny myself from some men in Muslim spaces. At the time, I wore a hijab, and I remember a specific incident where I was walking back to my dorm, late at night, and a guy who was in the MSA told me that the shirt that I was wearing was too short. I was quite taken aback when I heard that because, since I had never really been around Muslims, no one had ever questioned my modesty or my hijab before. Even my mom had never worn hijab, so she was never one that was very critical of the way that I dressed or anything. I was very taken aback, and I really didn't know how to process it. Consequently, after that incident, I started picking up more on such misogynistic comments and "jokes" that some Muslim men would just throw around.

As a result, towards the middle of the year, my friend and I decided to do a Halaqa on feminism in Islam and what that looks like. Halaqa is a kind of collective educational event where people discuss and learn about different topics within the context of Islam. We were very excited for it; we put in a lot of work, and overall, we were very happy with how the actual event went. We realized very quickly, however, that nothing seemed to change. It seemed like no matter what we did, no matter how many times we confronted these individual men or organized these events that openly discussed these problematic issues, the culture that already existed was not changing nor did it seem like it was going to. To this end, we felt that, as long as we stayed in these spaces and dedicated so much energy to these spaces, although it might make an inch of a difference, it would take so much from us and be extremely draining.

It was also traumatic to witness these instances of colorism, racism, sexism, and homophobia happening time and time again, whether it be to us or to our marginalized Muslim friends in these spaces that, ideally, were meant to be for us. Therefore, personally, seeing the trauma that was being inflicted on myself and my marginalized friends, in these spaces that I care about, pushed me farther and farther away from the Muslim community. And it was hard! It definitely was not easy because I did have friends in these Muslim spaces. Some were even leaders in these Muslim spaces, and it was really difficult to grapple with, "How am I supposed to enjoy my Muslim community and enjoy my Muslim friends while also being in these spaces that are so toxic and oppressive to members of their own community?"

Eventually though, I was pushed farther and farther away from Muslim communities, and even from my own Muslim identity and what that meant to me . It took me being very honest with myself and having this reconciliation of what it is about being Muslim that was important to me and what are the values that I hold as a Muslim American. Moreover, I had to understand that Muslim Americans have very diverse experiences, realizing that I'm not going to agree with every other Muslim American, and come to terms with it. Finally, I am trying to foster spaces with the Muslims whose values that I am motivated by, who bring me joy, and whom I agree with, and spaces that specifically prioritize marginalized Muslim American experiences.

Therefore, with all that in mind, some friends and I started this sort of biweekly event called "Fireside Chats," which, like the name suggests, consisted of a group of people just having a conversation. However, it revolved around topics that were considered controversial and/or taboo in the community, like dating, sexuality, mental health, et cetera. It was a different topic every time, and we were having all these conversations that we felt like were not happening in the "formal" Muslim spaces. It was very meaningful and helpful for a lot of people, including myself, but like with everything, there is a limit to how much impact mere conversation can bring, especially if not accompanied with some action. I think Fireside Chats was a great space; it was an informal space where people could have all these conversations about various topics without feeling judged or perhaps chastised for having "non-traditional" views. I believe conversations are a great place to start, especially in communities that have never had these conversations. However, we also sometimes get trapped in this idea of having a dialogue over and over again without seeing much tangible change.

To that end, during my third year, other Muslim students and I started forming this space, now known as Muslims United at UVA. We tried to re-imagine a space for Muslim students that prioritizes the experience of marginalized Muslims, that is inherently political, that fights for justice, and that resists against systems of oppression. We tried to form a space that prioritizes the collective healing of Muslims who not only live in this country that is Islamophobic, but also have been a part of Muslim spaces that were harmful and violent towards them.

Before going any further, I want to be clear that I am not the sole representative of MU as there is a whole variety of Muslim experiences in Muslims United. To explain the space itself, however, from the very conception, Muslims United was supposed to be a place for the most marginalized Muslims. We wanted to prioritize the experiences that we saw at UVA, at least the ones that we had known about, and the oppressions and harm they had faced in other Muslim spaces. We wanted to create this space that was specifically for them, where they are the leaders, the decision-makers, and people like me who do fit in the more normative Muslim American mold are in the back lines. We can do the labor and the work that is behind the scenes, but this space is fostered specifically for them, for marginalized Muslims. Not to say that other Muslims are not welcome—obviously we are—but we need to and will prioritize the feelings and experiences of Muslims who have been marginalized in other Muslim spaces to ensure that this space does not become one of those other ones that already exist.

We aimed to build the most perfect Muslim space: a space that we feel the safest, feel love, care, and the ability to be vulnerable and not scared, using the ideals that we learned from Islam of justice, and mercy, and kindness. We wanted to create a space that embodied all that! Therefore, with that in mind, we started simple, asking, "How do we want to feel in this space? What are the values we want to uphold?" We then went more into the logistics of, "What are the goals?" Given it inherently being a politicized space of marginalized Muslims from the very start, our goals were political. Also, fighting for justice is inherently part of Islam, so it is hard to find the divide between religious and political work. Nevertheless, we were very intentional and up-front with this space's political identity, saying, "Our existence is political at this university, and we do not want to fight against that. We understand that we are a political organization, and we want to use that power to fight for the liberation of and justice for other marginalized folks and ourselves."

Moreover, a very vital and central part of it was healing, using this space as a space where people who might have encountered harm or violence in other Muslim spaces would be treated differently and hence not feel that same way that they did in those others. It was definitely tricky trying to foster that space because even just entering a Muslim space after possibly having had traumatic experiences is difficult. Therefore, rebuilding that trust is something that we are also working towards, which is not easy and requires a lot of vulnerability from the people who come as well. It requires the cooperation of everyone involved, and it is a work in progress, but I strongly believe that it will be worth it all in the end.

White or white-passing Arab students and South Asians, including my own identity, like Pakistani, Indian, Bengalis. This specific group of the American Muslim population, compared to a lot of the other Muslim population in the United States including Black Muslims, Shia Muslims, etc., has a lot more power and privilege, even when we start from the very beginning and look at their immigration histories: their ability to come here, oftentimes, as technical workers rather than legacies of slavery or refugees being persecuted for their beliefs. Not to say that they don't overlap sometimes, but the majority of those experiences are faced by the minority within the marginalized group as opposed to those with aforementioned privileges. This further affects your experiences as a Muslim in the United States, it affects your wealth and your class, and it affects all those other things. Therefore, I think having organizations run by students who are the most privileged of this marginalized group makes it difficult for even more marginalized members of that group, for example queer Muslims or Black Muslims, to get a sense of belonging.

"BLACK MUSLIMS SHOULDN'T HAVE TO SPLIT THEMSELVES IN TWO: WE'RE BLACK AND MUSLIM, NOT EITHER/OR"

A.N.

A.N.'s narrative initiates consideration of the experience of being a Black Muslim in UVA's academic and social settings. A.N. discuss their experiences with their affinity groups, the MSA and the founding of the organization. Building on these insights, Black Muslim students at UVA discuss the experience of navigating the university, highlighting how difficult it can be to feel included and represented.

I really did not get involved with the Muslim Student Association (MSA) too much when I arrived on-Grounds. I had talked to the older students who told me how certain people in the organization can be racist or colorist. I'm the kind of person where I'll take in what people say, but I try really hard not to let it impact the way I view people. Still, I had that in mind when I went to MSA events. I did notice some issues. For instance, whenever I went to MSA events my first year, I didn't see my people. There were maybe two or three Black people there. One of the Black students was on the Executive Board and she would bring a couple of other people. Even then, though, they were East Africans. And for me, every time I would come to MSA events, they were also always the same East Africans who I already knew. I know for a fact that there are non-East African Black Muslims. I know for a fact they exist here at UVA. So that was frustrating because I was like, "I want to meet them." Then, during my second year, a friend and I went to a marshmallow night thing held by MSA in the Lawn room of one of the Executive Council members. We were roasting marshmallows and Arabic music was being played. And I was like, "This is weird. Why are you playing Arabic music when maybe two or three people out of everybody here speaks Arabic?" I mean, there were South Asian students as well as myself and my friend, who is Black. There were no religious connotations with the song, so you could just play English music. At that point, I began to feel there was not enough outreach to the Black Muslim community here on-Grounds, even though MSA was seeing itself as representing the diversity of Muslims at UVA. That really frustrated me.

My sense was that a lot of MSA members were growing frustrated. I remember the year before last when the MSA was debating whether it should participate in the "Trick or Treating on the Lawn." I understood the argument for not participating, but I was like "When did we decide that MSA was a Sunni organization that followed one type of way of thinking? That was never decided upon as a group." My understanding of the MSA was that it was a social club for Muslims to meet and get to know each other. Yet, here we are saying, "No, you can't do this thing. It's wrong." I'm like, "Who are you to dictate the way they practice Islam? It's not your job." I think people just kept feeling more and more frustrated.

Plus, there seemed to be a superiority complex within the Sunni of the South Asian and the Middle Eastern community in their view of Islam and the way that they move when participating in events that have the identity or the religion of Islam attached to it. In the MSA group chats, you can tell there are certain people who think they are the authority figure on how things are supposed to be done. They feel that everybody needs to hear their perspective, that their perspective is the only way. It makes it very frustrating for people who may not agree with the majority, don't follow the same path, or aren't as conservative as other Muslims at UVA. That is why there was a push to create our own spaces, a push to take back the power. It's like, why not? Why are we letting people dictate how we view Islam? I think that at UVA, the minority community pushes you to figure out what Islam means to you. I think that it's done unconsciously. You're like, dang, everybody is practicing Islam, everybody's "doing them" and nobody's trying to do anybody else. So it's like, "Dang, they're 'doing them,' I should be comfortable enough 'to do' me."

Finally, some students came up with a list of demands to reform MSA and presented it to the Executive Council. In response, MSA held a Town Hall meeting. At the meeting, people were explaining their grievances with MSA. But MSA had set it up so that everybody who had a grievance was on the right side, with everybody else on the left side or front. It was very divided. I remember this one girl who had not been at UVA as an undergraduate. It was her first year in the Medical School, and she was asking, "If you had a problem, why didn't you guys ever say anything?" We were all just sitting there like, "Babes, you just got here. You're not even in the GroupMe, so how are you going to be talking with your whole chest saying, 'Oh, you guys should have talked it out in the GroupMe.'" That was the mentality or the vibe surrounding MSA, so much superiority complex. It was at that moment, though, that Black Muslims at UVA and Muslim United at UVA began to emerge as new clubs. Muslims United was for all the minority Muslims, such as Queer, Shia, and so on. They're really focused on being there to support Muslim minorities, period. Black Muslims at UVA was specifically for Black Muslims.

Here's how Black Muslims at UVA began to form: I was with some of my Black Muslim friends who were trying to go to Jummah prayer at the local Masjid here, so the chaplain offered us a ride. We didn't realize she was the chaplain. We just thought she was a student because a lot of people in the GroupMe will write, "Oh, I'm going to the masjid at this time, if you need a ride, hit me up." So, we just hit her up, and it turned out she was the chaplain. During the ride, the conversation became about how there needs to be more Black representation in the Muslim community. One of the students said they worked at the Office of African American Affairs and said that the chaplain could reach out to the Black Muslim community through them. That led to the chaplain meeting with Black Muslims in her office and planning an OAAA event to talk about the history of Black Muslims in the US.

Those conversations, I believe, led to a discussion of whether there was a need for a Black Muslims club. For instance, if Black Muslims were not getting the resources they needed from MSA, maybe it was time to create our own organization. But the main goal was not the resources but to create a space where Black Muslims can come and identify who was another Black Muslim. It wouldn't matter how much of a Muslim you were or what kind of Muslim you were, that's literally not anyone's business. The club would just ask, "Do you identify with the Muslim community? Are you an ally for the Black Muslim community?" And if that's who you are, then, great. We want to know you. We want to be able to see you on-Grounds and be like, "Yo, that's a Black Muslim. That's what's up." So that was the goal. The club was just designed to create a social space for Black Muslims to just exist and be with people who know their struggles.

Forming the club, though, has been a slow process. It's hard. There's still a lot of members who are within the immigrant community. The more and more we work on it, though, the more we're meeting new people. I feel like we're getting exposure. At least the club has a lot more West African Muslims. I feel like I would not have met them without the club. It's slow going, but it's getting there. I think that if we continue to work and push over the next couple of years, the club will be strong. People also need to realize that Black Muslims are not trying to be an overly religious club. I think that if that's what people want to do, I'm sure the club can hold events that can cater to that need, but the club isn't trying to be your parent. It's literally just here to be a space for you to meet fellow Black Muslims and to have that community, that safe space. That's always been the goal of Black Muslims at UVA, to create a safe space for Black Muslims. And I want to say that when

Black Muslims at UVA was being formed, the MSA President reached out to help. The President would provide MSA resources to advertise our events, so there is a decent working relationship between the organizations. It's getting better at MSA, too, in terms of diversity. For instance, there is a member on the MSA Executive Council doing diversity outreach now, so they're making an effort.

With regards to being Black and Muslim in America, I feel like the US culture has made it seem as if Black Muslims don't exist outside of the immigrant community, which isn't true because Black Muslim culture has been here since slavery. I was talking to Dean Grimes, the associate dean at OAAA before she retired, and I was telling her, "I feel like the identity of being a Black Muslim doesn't exist anymore. I feel like that's not a common thing. It's shocking for me to meet a Black Muslim who isn't an immigrant." She was like, "What really?" She grew up in the time where it was normal to have Black Muslims as relatives, knowing who they are. It wasn't a rarity, I guess. She was like, "Yeah, for me, growing up, it was normal to have your uncle, your cousin or someone you're related to be a Muslim." That intermixing was there. I was like, "That must have been then, because now, it's a lot harder to see Black Muslims who aren't immigrants if you're not in certain cities. If you're not in Baltimore, if you're not in Chicago, Philly, or New York. Outside of those communities, it's hard to see them."

I was in a UVA office, and the staff there would be talking to each other. When doing so, it was just so easy for them to drop in Christian phrases and word choices casually in conversations. Christianity just easily flows through the conversations. I don't feel comfortable using Islamic phrases in my day-to-day conversations unless I was talking to another Muslim. I've never been like, "Oh, Alhamdulillah." I would never say that unless I knew the other person was also Muslim. But for the office staff, they would just say, "Jesus Christ." It just made me feel uneasy because it gives the presumption that Christianity is the default religion if one is Black, which detracts from Islam's history and presence within the Black culture. My whole thing was that Black Muslims shouldn't have to split themselves in two, like "If I'm Black, then my Muslim identity has to disappear. If I'm Muslim, then my Black identity has to disappear." Now for me, this splitting is not an option because I'm a hijabi, so you're going to get both. Yet, Christianity and Christian culture is so ingrained into the Black community here at UVA. I think people have this idea that if you're Black, then you're Christian, but the Black identities, in terms of religion, are very diverse.

Islam was a huge part of Black culture back in the day. People don't realize just how ingrained Islam was within the Black community, that a lot of the things within the Black culture have Islamic history to them. For instance, the "Philly Beard" has its roots tied to the Islamic practice, a Sunnah, of growing one's beard, and it was Black Muslims in Philly that set that trend. Moreover, if you look at the history of jazz, hip-hop, and a lot of these other things that are strongly associated with Black culture, you'll be surprised at just how much of the Muslim culture and Black Muslims had influenced, shaped, and contributed to it. Unfortunately, however, this isn't common knowledge nor do you see Islam's presence within the Black community as pervasively as you once would. A big reason behind why we no longer see it, I believe, has to do with the mainstream media and its depiction of Islam as a thing to be feared. When the media started its fearmongering, the Islam within the Black community started being hidden. People, consciously or unconsciously, started hiding "their Islam," probably as a survival mechanism. As a result, Islam slowly ceased being a celebrated part of the Black culture. It probably further led to the current misinformed notion that Christianity is the only, or at least the main, religion associated with being Black. I feel like the atmosphere at UVA is continuing that idea, too: that if you're black, you're Christian. In that way, the Black Muslims at UVA CIO brings awareness to the Black Muslim identity and its rich history.

Having more qualified Black Muslim professors would also help bring awareness to our identity, our heritage. The atmosphere at UVA is constructed very much through the white man's gaze, meaning that everything is through their perspective. A lot of the classes do tend to be taught by white professors, so there is almost that gaze built into the class from the onset. I think my first year at UVA, a Black Muslim professor was hired, but clearly more Black Muslim professors should be on faculty. Even in terms of professors who represent Islam, it's not really happening. Maybe the language department has one or two professors who are Muslim, and that's it. But there is no doubt that the numbers are small.

With the Global Development Studies (GDS), I think there's a more holistic perspective than in other departments because the students push for it. The students are unafraid to call out Islamophobia or Islamophobic-influenced views. I think GDS, in terms of the student population, is pretty diverse. There's not a lot of us, but the ones that are there, we're not all the same. We're all different, which I think is really great. I would say in terms of the teachers within the program, I'm not really sure. I can guess confidently that there's not a lot of Muslim faculty. In general, GDS has a very US-focused public policy perspective. Everything's from an American point of view with regards to class content and how they're taught. The same thing goes for the way people view Islam. No one's outwardly explicitly Islamophobic, but you hear the traces of it in terms of the way that they push policies or present opinions.

Finally, when the white professors teach Islamic classes, they should be sure to not just teach them from the Arab perspective or the South Asian perspective. Muslim history is not just confined to those two communities/societies. Muslim history is within Africa. And not just North Africa, it's within West Africa. It's within East Africa; it's within Central Africa. Professors need to teach those histories as well as the history of Islam within South America, within Asia. They need to teach Islam within the period of slavery and before slavery in what became the United States. That's what I would want. And I'm not going to be like, "He/She needs to be a Black Muslim to teach the course." As long as the professor is qualified, then teach it. I guess that's the biggest thing I would want from UVA is to give more opportunities to teach the broader history of Islam.

It is important to really understand the Black Muslim community. It's important to learn about Black Muslim culture because I think that we're a great example of the diversity and history of Islam. It's not just the Nation of Islam and Muhammad Ali. That's not all there is to being a Black Muslim. It's a lot more complicated. I also think it's a great example of what the Islamic community should be like, which is diverse, which is "you do you." You practice Islam the way that *you* believe is right to practice Islam, because at the end of the day, Islam is between you and Allah and nobody else. As much as it is a communal religion, Islam is still an individual religion. You have to "do you!" You can guide people; you can advise them and tell them what you think is right, but at the end of the day, you can't control them, nor should you. I think that's what the Black Muslim community is like at UVA. With the young community, that's how we move, for the most part.

Omer Gorashi
Class of 2021
University of Virginia School of Architecture

When it comes to the idea or understanding of being Black and Muslim, a lot of other people, whether they be Muslim or non-Muslim, think that there's only a very small number of us, but that is not the reality at all. Looking at African American history, for example, here in the US, there's a lot of Muslim narratives that get left out. Thinking of people like Malcolm X—he had been very much influenced by Sudanese Imams and sheikhs, which then led him from the Nation of Islam to Islam.

With regards to MSA, for me, just because I'm in the Architecture school, I just never had as much time to participate in it to a great extent. Hearing from other students, however, there's been a number of things: from them not feeling comfortable to there not being the same level of consideration for them as compared to what's given to Arab or Desi members. Sometimes there even have been kind of outright problematic and insensitive comments. Some members even make Black jokes, and I, myself, have experienced being around people just casually saying the N-word, and it's made me pretty uncomfortable, to be honest. And even if someone speaks up or confronts them about it, they brush it off saying, "Oh, you know that I'm only joking." You know things like these, where to some it can seem very small, but for others, it could be the reason why they are not part of MSA anymore.

To their credit, the MSA is really trying to improve on that aspect, which I've been very pleased to see. Be that as it may, however, I'm glad that there's now some sort of space for just Black Muslim students, just because there are a lot of similarities among Black Muslims. There are similar things that we go through as Muslim students in general, but at the same time, there's still these slight differences and nuances within being Muslim. And with this space, it's about celebrating being both Black and Muslim.

There are minorities within the Muslim minority. I had a friend, and we were just talking one evening in the A-School and he was like, "Oh, Omer, it must be crazy for you." I was like, "What is?" And he said, "You're, like, a quadruple minority." I responded, "What do you mean?" He's like, "You're Black. You're Muslim. You're an immigrant. You're technically Middle Eastern. So, you find yourself having to deal with almost always being not only an odd one out but being slightly different in almost each and every one of those circles." I mean, he's right, but personally, I think it's pretty cool. Nonetheless, there are times where I will begin to notice those things slightly. Say I'm with a group of friends that are African American rather than African, or I might be with Muslim friends who are all Desi or Arab, in those instances, I guess it makes you realize that you don't fit neatly into any one of these groups.

With the larger UVA, I'd say here on-Grounds there's nothing, at least, that I, myself, have experienced where I felt that there's an outward intolerance of me being Muslim. There are times, however, where I have felt like I was not being considered. For instance, in our department whenever there are social events, there always has to be drinking; I don't know why. Like, this one time there was this professional event in New York. During our trip to visit the city, we visited an office during the day, and that evening, there was an event for us students to meet alumni and people in that office. But then of course, they bring in drinking. So then, everyone was like, "Oh, you should go ahead and grab a drink." It was me and another student that was Muslim, and we were just like, "Oh no, we don't want to deal with not only the alcohol but also just having to see classmates, faculty, and alumni intoxicated." So we just left. It's things like these that make you feel a certain way, where it's not necessarily outwardly intolerant or discriminatory, but just inconsiderate. Like this was meant to be a professional, networking event, and although it was supposed to have an informal vibe, it would be nice if organizers kept in mind that there might be students who don't partake in alcohol, and we should not have to miss out on such opportunities merely because we don't drink. And I am not saying that all events should ban alcohol for our sake, but, again, it's that assumption where the default understanding is that everybody drinks, and if you don't, you're just the outlier who will miss out even in departmental professional events.

I'm here to help, however I can. Although I, myself, may not have something in particular that I want to share, the least I can do is be a part of something that's larger, even if it just merely adds to what another person has shared. And all of our shared experiences together can then maybe get the school's attention through this work. The fact that you're doing this, I'm already like, "Okay! There are people that are working towards getting Muslims heard, getting Black Muslims heard and represented!"

Fadumo Hussein
Class of 2023
College of Arts and Sciences

I personally am not aware of the biases that my peers, professors, or campus members have. And when I do talk to at least my professors, I feel there's a pretty good understanding. None of my professors seem to be judgmental of me or where I come from. They challenge me academically, but I'm up for the challenge. I've never really had a negative interaction with them or anything of that manner. I think with my peers and campus members, this has more to do with my identity beyond being a Muslim. But I've noticed a lot of people have been like, "Oh, you seem intimidating," or whenever I do get upset and I assert myself and my feelings, it's always, "Oh, you seem, like, aggressive" when it's clearly taken out of context, and had it been someone who isn't a Black woman who reacted in a similar way, it would have been taken as that person simply expressing their feelings.

I think the responses I receive have to do with the fact that I am Black. I guess being a Black Muslim, there's also those weird spaces in religious-based organizations, like the MSA, where if I basically seem like I'm doing what any normal Muslim would do, there's this weird sense of, "Oh, I'm so proud of you!" I don't know how to articulate it, but I remember going to Jummah once and I was talking to someone. They seemed really proud of my being there and, now looking back, definitely surprised. And I know back at home or where I live, there's a very large Arab and South Asian population, and there's a lot of anti-Blackness within those communities. And I feel like it trickled down to the sense of Islam that, "Oh, when you think of Muslims, you think of Arabs and South Asians," but 1 in 3 Black people are Muslim.

In a way, I feel like in those spaces I have to prove that I'm Muslim by saying, "Oh, I pray." But a lot of people are like, "Oh, that's so great of you" and, like, I understand the general good job with doing it, but at the end of the day, I am nineteen. It's an expectation and there's this weird level of "I'm going to put you on a pedestal, and I'm going to praise you because you're so amazing." Or say, if for some reason, I'm not praying, I didn't pray five times a day and if this does catch wind, it's always, "She's not, like, a good Muslim. She's not a real Muslim." I feel like that statement—it's rude. Its roots come from this idea, like anti-blackness and not really recognizing the Black Muslim as a full Muslim. I think this is something that I first noticed outside of the university back in my hometown. I guess if I were to come back and say that I'm actively involved with the Muslim community or the MSA here, it would be like, "Wow, we're so proud of you," "Wow, we didn't know people like you could do that," or whatever.

I think this attitude is quite prevalent among the Muslim community, especially in those who are non-Black Muslims. I think it's something that was influenced by colonialism with this idea of white being the best, knowing that, for example, many South Asians participate in skin bleaching because they see a darker complexion as something that's not acceptable. It's basically colorism, and that can trickle down into beliefs and stuff like that and how they interact with others who aren't like them in those same belief systems. I try to make sure that when I come to UVA that I always bring notice to people that say, "Yeah, I'm proud of being Black, I'm proud of being Muslim, and I'm proud of being Somali in particular in terms of ethnicity." That's something I learned to carry with pride in high school. So, I guess I don't really feel I'm living sort of a double life; I'm more of advocating for those who aren't here and trying to make space for them if they choose to come here in the future. I'm trying to make a space where they do not feel like they have to start explaining their entire livelihoods from the get-go. I'm pretty consistent about how proud I am of my identity as a whole and how I advocate for those identities.

"A HUGE PART OF BEING MUSLIM IS ALSO ADVOCATING FOR THE RIGHTS OF THOSE THAT ARE UNDERREPRESENTED AND OPPRESSED"

Saqib Rizvi
Class of 2021
School of Engineering and Applied Sciences

Saqib Rizvi's narrative invites the reader into the experience of being a leader within the UVA Muslim Student Association (MSA). In particular, Rizvi discusses how one of his main objectives was to provide programming and social events that appealed to parts of the Muslim student community that might not typically feel included in the MSA. Rizvi also discusses how MSA has worked to improve as an organization through efforts such as Housing and Residence Life and Interfaith Student Center and the support of the UVA administration in these efforts.

At first, I didn't really know whether I wanted to join Muslim Student Association because there's the stereotype out there, "It's another brown club. It's not very diverse. It's where you just meet other people that look like you." Even after joining during my first year, I grew a little distant from the organization. I spent my time hanging with friends from my residence hall. Like a lot of students, they partied on the weekends. You know, the usual stuff. I gradually realized that I couldn't take part in these activities because of my Muslim identity. I started feeling as if I was normalizing a part of American culture that wasn't a part of my religious identity. So, I ended up returning to the MSA and making friends, which helped me adjust. Instead of feeling lonely on Friday and Saturday nights when my friends went to parties, through MSA I found an alternative to that stereotypical narrative—that partying is the only way you can socialize with others. Ultimately, growing a little distant from MSA helped me understand the importance of the organization.

Now that I'm President of MSA (2020-21), I have been thinking a lot about how the organization could be perceived as self-segregating. I think we can provide programming that appeals to people of different demographics. We heard that MSA members wanted more than just programming. They wanted to hear about topics that are not just specific to Muslims but rather programming that addresses diversity or that talks about the different viewpoints on Islam. There are specifically verses, even in the Quran, that promote this focus on diverse narratives such as, "We made you into different tribes so that you may know one another." Our members wanted an opportunity to learn about each other, in all their diversity of thoughts and interests. For that reason, a significant goal of MSA last year was to collaborate with an organization started by community members at our local mosque, the Islamic Society of Central Virginia (ISCV). That organization is called "Li Ta'arafu" which started from the desire to "know one another" and also literally translates to the same phrase. They have events where a certain culture or heritage is highlighted. Then they invite individuals from that culture to share aspects of the culture such as cuisine, traditions, clothing, etc. It's just a really good way of building conversation and learning about each other. We sponsored similar events last year, as well as invited speakers, but, again, COVID has hindered those programs from being well attended. But that's just the issue we'll have to continue to battle this coming semester. I really hope, though, we will continue to incorporate different topics within our speaker programming in the future.

In fact, I decided to run for President of MSA in response to what happened in 2019. When the letter came out charging MSA with not being inclusive, it was surprising because that year's Council was one of the most inclusive. We were improving in our programming and topics being discussed. It was during my second year that we started to see a shift with regards to the topics we brought up as an MSA community. I think we invited various speakers who spoke to more than just the regular Desi Muslim experience. Honestly, I gained perspectives that I didn't have before. I still keep up with some of the speakers and I'm hoping that we can invite them back this year. So, I feel like the letter represented more so a buildup of frustration from past years than an acute response to a specific event, finally culminating in the events of last year. It was clear that a lot of our Muslim brothers and sisters did not feel included within the larger MSA community. That issue needed to be addressed.

My primary goal as President, then, was to have programming focused on conversation and dialogue regarding tough issues, like inclusion, to focus on how the MSA community can improve. My hope was that if we can have these conversations, we can work on improving our community as a whole by making it more inclusive and representative. Even prior to my term, previous Councils implemented changes in our constitution to combat this same issue by ensuring that if there are bigoted voices within the Muslim community, then we could remove them from MSA. Building an inclusive and caring community, then, was the main issue I wanted to tackle. I recognize that there will always be more work to do. Some elements of our community will always feel the need for greater representation. That's something I've come to realize through the leadership of the MSA — problems always come up. I believe, though, that we always need to listen to those voices and then figure out whether there is something fundamentally wrong with the MSA structure. If so, we should fix it. Sometimes that has been the case.

For example, I know last year a lot of people were opposed to the form-ing of a Black Muslim CIO just because they felt that the community would become more fragmented. In retrospect, the idea of the Black Muslim CIO has been very beneficial. I feel like Black Muslims do need to have their own space where they feel comfortable. That's what the CIO has provided. They provided that community a space where people can feel welcome and not feel judged. And I've realized that regardless of how much we might try at MSA, I feel like Black Muslims might not feel as welcome as they might like, or we hope they feel. It was hard to come to terms with that as an organization, but I'd say that supporting a space for them is honestly one of the best things we can do as an organization. My hope is that we can provide support through avenues such as advertising or funding. They can provide programming that we might never think of providing. And the people who are part of this orga-nization can also benefit from the programming the MSA provides. It's just about increasing options.

Still, I think a lot of good has happened as a result of the letter. It's been hard to see a lot of it, but in retrospect, the community on-Grounds has be-come more cognizant of their actions. There are a lot more people that want to learn about different perspectives, different topics. I'm really excited for next semester because we have invited a speaker to talk about sexual health within the Muslim community. That's something that's not really addressed. We're just trying our best to talk about different things that might not nec-essarily be what you think is the stereotypical brown Muslim topics. I don't know what you would qualify as such topics, probably marriage or something like that.

So, I know this year's Council has been phenomenal in regard to the programming they want to put out. It's just with COVID-19, a lot of stuff has been hard to program. The one good thing I'd say we've achieved despite CO-VID is recruitment of the first-years. Even though this year's first-year's class has been the most unfortunate with regards to social interaction and meet-ing friends that are Muslims, I think the Big Sib Little Sib (BSLS) program that we've done, even on Zoom, has been amazing. I've gotten to meet a lot of first-years that I wouldn't have met otherwise. That has been really good. Even with the challenges of COVID, we've been able to get a lot of first-years involved within the organization, so I'm excited to see where that goes with the coming year.

A lot of people think that our role is mainly as a religious organization, but I'd like to argue otherwise. I feel like a huge part of being Muslim is also advocating for the rights of those that are under-represented and oppressed. In many ways, MSA is also a political organization. I know this past semester we did work regarding Uyghur human rights. We held a conversation with the Jewish Leadership Council. I thought the event was successful. I think we try to release statements whenever something happens. So I feel like MSA does have the capacity to also be a political organization, and there is definitely more we can do as an organization. At the same time, however, I would say some people on Council don't really view the organization as one that is political.

Outside of MSA, when I consider the number of Muslims on-Grounds, I would say the representation in a lot of student organizations needs to be improved. There are certain student organizations that do a really good job recruiting with Muslims, such as Housing and Residence Life (HRL). There are a lot of RAs (Resident Advisors) who are Muslim, a change that I've seen occur just throughout my time at UVA. For instance, in my first year, I knew of maybe five or six Muslims within HRL. I think this has been with the advent of MILE, though; a lot of people have started to get involved more and more within different student organizations. So HRL has become a huge hub for a lot of Muslims. I feel like that's a really good thing, mainly because if you're a Muslim student as a first year and you have a Muslim RA that's there for you as a mentor, then you have someone you can go to for advice with stuff pertaining to the Muslim experience at UVA. It does help build that self-esteem, that narrative that you don't have to conform to the normal UVA experience that is advertised.

I have talked to a lot of people in the senior leadership of organizations, such as Honor and UJC and Student Council. They've agreed there is a need to do a better job at recruiting from minority organizations as well as acknowledging that the Muslim community is one of those communities that they haven't done a good job with in the past. I believe the value of having Muslims in a variety of organizations is that you might be much more comfortable reaching out about joining, getting help with how to prepare the application, and seeking advice on how to interview effectively. We've tried to overcome this lack of representation through recruitment of students for these organizations through MSA. Initially, my hope was to hold a career fair or club fair within the MSA, but obviously, we were unable to do that because of COVID. Hopefully, in the future, we can do better getting Muslim students engaged and have their voices be heard within different student organizations.

I do want to give credit to UVA for the Interfaith Center that they funded through the Multicultural Student Center this past year. That was a huge step towards making Muslim students feel that they're valued. Before the Interfaith Center, we only had a very, very small room to pray. A huge part of the Muslim student experience is finding a place to pray during your time on-Grounds. And just that one thing, creating the Center, created a place for Muslim students to just come out and hang out. Not even just to go there to pray. People came up there to eat and socialize. I thought the Center was an amazing thing. So, props to UVA for actually focusing on this issue. But again, there are other steps that can be taken, such as providing accommodations to Muslims during Ramadan. A lot of students don't really know that they can get accommodations, but a lot of professors are very understanding. They will support you. Still, if UVA was cognizant of that issue, students wouldn't have to go out of their way and ask their professors about accommodations. It would just be a given.

UVA has also made some strides in deliberately including the Muslim community in more programs and events. There's a leadership retreat called L2K that's been a part of the UVA student self-governance leadership since the year 2000. Recently, they've started to include the MSA as part of this leadership retreat. It's been very nice to see that they value the Muslim community enough to invite us. Also, I am currently acting on the Lawn Selection Committee as the representative for the MSA. We basically act as application readers to advocate for Muslims that are applying, ensuring they have a better chance of getting accepted. It's nice to see that UVA is making some sort of effort at being inclusive to the different minority communities. Because it's not just the MSA, it's a lot of other minority CIOs as well that UVA is making sure to include.

"BEING COMFORTABLE IN A SPACE MEANS WELCOMING SINCERITY OVER COMFORMITY"

M.M.

M.M.'s narrative initiates a consideration of being a Queer Muslim at UVA and the need to find affinity groups with whom to share such experiences. Particular attention is paid to the difference between being religiously or culturally Muslim. In the process, M.M. discusses how the work of creating such safe spaces necessarily exists within a history of diverse experiences at UVA, which creates possibilities and complications within the university's LGBT community. As such, the following narrative articulates the nuances and intersectional experiences of this important Muslim community.

I didn't get along with my parents. I came out to my dad's wife, my stepmother. She was super homophobic. As a result, I left home when I was a senior in high school. I was still in touch with my father. He wasn't exactly accepting either, unfortunately, but it's okay. Though we were distant for a while, today we're very close. But I couldn't go home, so having a stable community was so important to me. Sometimes I literally just needed a place to call home. I needed a space that captured the full aspect of who I was as a person. It mattered a lot to have a stable community that captured the full me.

And I found that space at Hereford Residential College. I guess I found a space and I didn't look anywhere else. Since I was coming into UVA as a financially independent student, I didn't have a place to stay during the holidays most of the time. Residential colleges let you stay during the winter break; I chose that space partly for that. Initially, that was a good chunk of the reason. However, I also liked the fact that I can be with first to fourth years in that space. I grew to like the fact that it was a different kind of social space, more than just party culture, more than just, like, frat stuff. I'm not judging those spaces. Some people find those spaces meaningful and that's a good thing, too. But for me, it wasn't my space. I'm not a big party person. I'm also not super religious, so I sometimes drink but very rarely. For me, I wanted a space that you can be yourself, where you can just have other kinds of partying. Hereford's residential space made sense for my context, so I guess I just chose quality of being active in one space, over quantity of being involved in many clubs. I chose to give my whole to this one space. That's the decision I made. I decided to fully engage in that community.

I think my time at Hereford represented a lot of what was most important to me about my experience at UVA. I have to go back to freshman year, going to a social event, people playing horror games and eating snacks, in the space known as the Hereford Hub, the student space. People were just having a good time. I was being my goofy self. But, yeah, I'm really quirky and I lean into that identity. I'm very unapologetic about being quirky, being myself. In that space, I felt so comfortable just being quirky. I didn't question who I was. I didn't feel like anyone questioned me as a person. Everyone was just doing their thing. People from so many different backgrounds. You have the people who are in the frats. You have the people who are just focused on studies all the time, and that's okay, too. You have people who do other things in between or altogether different. Just everyone's doing their thing. It's a welcoming space. That was the one moment that captured my experience at UVA. That's also because I chose to be in that space on purpose. I don't know if I had chosen an alternative route if I would have had a different experience.

For me, I found being comfortable at UVA simply meant more voices, more diversity, to be honest. It seemed to come down to that for me. I would say being comfortable in a space means welcoming *sincerity* over *conformity* because a lot of spaces at UVA, at least sometimes, tend to focus more on the latter—conformity—and this probably just comes with being at a competitive highly-ranked school. I also felt my major, computer science, was sometimes big on conformity. People talked so much about grades and talked so much about what internship you obtained. Within such a conforming, stressful academic culture, my very little understanding of the Muslim clubs at the time was that they were also conforming, that they leaned towards conservative Muslim ideas of doing things. And my sense about the traditional queer spaces was that these spaces were also leaning toward conforming to certain ideas of queer culture.

I didn't always feel welcome in the traditional queer spaces of UVA. I didn't quite fit into the established clubs (Queer Student Union and Sigma Omicron Rho) that were the most prominent LGBTQ+ clubs at UVA. These clubs have their own culture, its own social performances. I think different spaces have their own performance aspects. It's just a natural part of being a social cultural space as well. Performance expectations exist in the mainstream UVA queer community. They exist in the mainstream UVA Muslim community, in the frat communities, and in the academic communities. It might be the way you dress, it might be the way you talk or what you talk about. And I felt my beliefs didn't necessarily fit neatly into a number of other spaces at UVA, including some queer or Muslim spaces. I didn't feel like I could be myself in several of the established queer spaces at the time I was an undergrad, nor in the established Muslim spaces. But for some reason, because I felt conformity wasn't a big issue at Hereford, since it's not a place where people need to conform as much to any particular thing or tradition, I felt like I fit in. It's just "Be yourself." Everyone's just chilling.

In some weird way, Hereford's culture can be perceived in a bit of a negative light. It's lack of a conformist culture makes people ask, "What is the mission of Hereford?" There is a mission, but it's not as strong on the social side. And for me, that's a good thing. Hereford should be understood as being a space where you can be yourself. Just be yourself. Bring that to the social space at Hereford. It's less focused on conformity and more focused on just being sincere to who you are as a person. Tell your truth unapologetically in that space, and your truth will be welcome. As long as it's not hurting anybody else, your truth is welcome. Such spaces accommodate different voices.

The Muslim community is so diverse. I think traditionally Muslim spaces tend to value tradition that in some ways is powerful, a good thing. At times, though, such spaces can be harmful for some people. Pragmatically, I don't think it is a bad idea to have spaces where Muslims of the same background or understanding of Islam can get together. I don't know how to explain it, exactly, but I would say it's about having space in that community for people who don't practice as much, people who have different opinions, people who practice their Islam differently, and then letting them be in control of that space.

Whether it's queer Muslims or less religious Muslims. Whether it's Black Muslims, South Asian Muslims, Arabs. Any kind of Muslim, really. Certain backgrounds can cultivate their own space. Those people should not be expected to always present themselves as the arbiter for change. It's a lot of pressure. They should have their own space. A shared space might put a lot of pressure on those people from the minority backgrounds or the less represented backgrounds to put in energy to try to change or to try to move the cultural window toward the opinion of different voices. It can be exhausting. I would have a space for everyone to come together, to just be yourself. Honestly, it could be as simple as just coming to the space, be yourself, but also have the spaces for some identities, like Black Muslims, to just be among themselves. Having more space like that is not necessarily a bad thing, in my opinion. You can coexist in both spaces.

And this is where my pragmatic side kicks in: you could bring these communities together. I don't know if you could change the fact that some people are going to be more liberal and that some are going to be more conservative in Muslim spaces. But having a space where different groups of Muslims can mix together, putting aside social expectation, putting aside religious expectation, just having a space where you can say you're Muslim among a diverse and full representation of that community, I believe that would be powerful. And it could be any kind of flavor of Muslim. You can be just culturally Muslim, maybe you even drink and eat pork. I don't care. If you identify as Muslim. Fine, come to this space. If you are a hijabi, if you're not even a Muslim but just curious about the religion. Fine come to this space. You're welcome to. I think there's so many different truths, maybe just accepting that, at the end of the day, it's between you and your God. I'm not saying people who believe that one has to have certain social or cultural ideas to be a good Muslim have to stop making that argument. They can still do that. If it's their truth, if it's valuable to them, no one should stop them from following that. But at the same time, Muslims have never been homogenous. It's always been a very diverse community. To be blunt, I'll get straight to the point, it's just having a space where people can feel comfortably themselves without judgment on how much they practice their religion. Let's just try to create a space where that can exist.

I'll give you an example. I didn't feel comfortable being in the Queer Student Union (QSU) at UVA. I don't perform a certain way. I don't dress a certain way. I don't go to as many queer clubs and queer events. It's not that I'm not queer. It doesn't mean I'm less queer than the queer people who get really involved and attend more mainstream UVA queer events than I do. Just because I'm, like, not as involved in UVA's mainstream queer clubs (QSU and SOR is what I imagine to fit this label) doesn't mean I'm not queer or less queer. Just because I'm not practicing a lot as a Muslim doesn't mean I'm not Muslim.

I can't say much about representation within MSA. I have not been actively involved in MSA during my time at UVA. Part of it was that there was also a bit of hearsay about homophobic statements being made in those spaces, that those spaces can be kind of conservative—that had some effect. I also had some people in that space actively reach out to me, though. They wanted me to be a part of it, knowing I'm a queer Muslim, and that did mean a lot to me. That tells me that there were efforts to try to welcome, to change, MSA. There were efforts to make MSA more welcoming.

When I was a first-year or second year at UVA, I actually remember going to an MSA barbecue. It's interesting because I think I've always been more of a cultural Muslim. I'm not super religious. Maybe I associate the MSA space to be more religious. I didn't feel like I could talk about the same things because I'm not as religious. I don't know. I couldn't have as many religious conversations because I'm not super religious. That's okay to have spaces where people can be religious, less religious. That's not a bad thing. It was just at that moment, MSA didn't fully capture who I was, the full person. It was like one part of me was not the full person. It's not like we talked about something serious or super conservative the whole time, but I just felt like I wanted to invest my time into a space that can capture the full me, I guess, just because I had limited time.

There was a time where I got to know some queer Muslims. It was informal. We did PULSE together. PULSE is about dialogues. It's almost like bootcamp; it's over a short period of time, but it gets very intense. It's a very emotional experience. It's like a more condensed intense version of Sustained Dialogue, but it's essentially the same thing. A lot of PULSE people end up going to Sustained Dialogue, by the way. So, it's essentially the same beast, the same kind of thing. I met some queer Muslims at PULSE, and we got to know each other. We got acquainted. We talked a little bit about being a queer Muslim, but we didn't go into depth. It was just very informal, but it was nice. It was just nice to be able to say, "Hey, I know a queer Muslim. That's cool. I'm not the only one." It was nice in that way.

My first thought was that there are so many kinds of Muslims. It might be a slow process, but I think that my word of advice is to find other queer Muslims. That's a good place to start. I don't know if queer Muslims are comfortable going public. I just don't know very many, but there are definitely some. It's a hard place to be because you don't want to out anybody, right? I would say, "Start with people you know." People who are open about being queer and they're also open about being Muslim. Go to them. Personally, I think it's okay to be chatting in a friendly way and be like, "Hey, I'm curious. Would you want to spearhead this space?" Maybe just an everyday conversation. People who you know are friends with queer Muslims, that's a good place to start. Those people being openly queer or, maybe, even if they're not open, which is fine, the space can start out as confidential.

Maybe it might be hard to engage in the wider community at first. No one's going to put the burden on you to shoulder the pressure of changing the community or not changing. Just be yourself, find other queer Muslims.

That's a good place to start if people are worried about coming out, very simply. If you are afraid of coming out and you want to come out, a good place to start is to find other queer Muslims, talk to them informally. Just acquaint yourself with them.

I think from there, you can ideate about how to create something bigger. Perhaps, first work with infrastructure that exists, clubs and organizations that exist, create your space, whether it's through MSA, through QSU, help with advice from other queer religious clubs. Start simply. Don't feel too much pressure to change the world, I guess. Find just a space for others like you and talk to them informally. I think that's how a lot of these liberal activist movements start, whether they're talking about queer movements, Black liberation movements, women's rights movements, and other kind of movements. Find other people who are like you, like-minded and it doesn't have to necessarily be formal. It can be informal and that's a good place to start. Just find a friend. That's it.

I feel this pause when I think about queer Muslim spaces at UVA. Perhaps, the pause shows how my opinion about the UVA space is like MSA, in being a very conservative space. I almost feel uncomfortable suggesting things. Ideally, you could start a sub-section for queer Muslims by queer Muslims. If it's possible to start such a space, I think that'll be helpful. I also think that would be a very controversial idea. I could be wrong; I don't know. I haven't been active enough there to know how things have changed and how things have developed. The current MSA just feels so strongly conservative to me that I almost feel uncomfortable simply suggesting changes. I'm not sure it's a bad thing, but I come from a place where I feel uncomfortable making people uncomfortable. I don't want to bring down people's idea about their Islam. I recognize, though, how the Muslim community has become tied to some aspects of seeing gayness as a sin and has been traditionally so strongly anti-gay. In that context, if someone suggests ways to actively include queer Muslim students openly in the organization, they can be heard as saying "MSA is anti-Muslim." It feels that way, but it shouldn't be that way. But there just seems to be such a lack, in my opinion, of a truly liberal Muslim space that it's hard to even start such a conversation. It's a bit like Muslims United and the Black Muslims, I would support those spaces, personally. If I was present in MSA, I'd be like, "Heck. Look. You all do your thing. Let's work together. You got your space. You come out." It's like welcoming other spaces for Muslims.

I don't think it's a threat against MSA. I think such a group could be under the umbrella of MSA; it can be a sibling group to MSA. I think MSA should welcome such spaces, in whatever form it seems appropriate for people who are queer Muslims. The goal is to support spaces where they can be together and can talk about what it's like being queer Muslim. Create and allow those spaces to exist. Reach out to queer Muslims. Just be the student group that asks, "Hey, we want you to feel welcome. What do you want?" Letting queer Muslims decide what space they want then making that space.

And honestly, I would say talk to QSU about how to start this work. Talk to the LGBTQ center. Tell them, "Hey, they want to start a queer Muslim space. Do you know queer Muslims?" Maybe they can work with MSA and other Muslim spaces to find queer Muslims and create that space. And QSU is very, very good about creating confidential spaces since a good amount of queer people care about confidentiality. In fact, from my understanding, QSU creates confidential meetings, confidential spaces for people who are queer and don't want to be out because that is such an important sensitivity for queer people, traditionally speaking. So, I would say talk to QSU. See if they can use the skills they have, the experience they have of creating those spaces that are safe and welcoming to them, to create a space that's Muslim and queer. Maybe it's a project to work on with other clubs that already work with queer spaces. I think it's a very pragmatic way of doing it. You work with existing stuff, infrastructure to make it actualized. I think it's the quickest way to make it actualized, start the work within spaces that already exist. That brings up another point. The queer Christian clubs at UVA can also be consulted to see how they're doing it. That might be a good middle ground. They might have suggestions on how to balance the two sides of the coin.

I saw a TED Talk by Chimamanda Ngozi Adichie called "The Danger of a Single Story." Adiche talks about how understandings of Africans are based on Western narratives. This is the case not only in the Western world and, by extension, the outside world, but even within Africa itself. If all you hear is this single story of Africa, you can't help but have the first thing that comes to mind be that "single story" when Africa is mentioned. Adiche is arguing that when people are presented with different stories, they then can form a more nuanced and more multidimensional idea of Africa, of people from Africa. And that's just one example. So now, what about Muslims and the Muslim world? Same idea. It's like we've been told a single story on Islam, on Muslims, by the media. And people speaking up in a space like an academic space, speaking up to create a dialogue is important. They haven't heard a different story yet. So it definitely helps a lot to hear a different story from Muslim students and just different Muslims in class.

I've always wanted to explore these different, disparate, intersectional identities in the Muslim community specifically. We talked mostly about the queer spaces, intersectionality of queer and Muslim space, but also I'm not super religious. I think, though, Islam allows us a space to encourage certain things that I think are valuable. I think there are some values in Islam that are valuable. In a weird way, instead of taking values from Islam from the inside out, my belief and religious identity have fluctuated a lot. Sometimes I felt like I was "religiously" not religious, even sometimes atheist. I'm still Muslim culturally, though. I've never rejected that part of my cultural heritage. I've always felt it was important. It's the way I engaged with that heritage that changed. It wasn't always from a religious perspective. Sometimes it was from a religious perspective, other times it was from a cultural perspective. In some ways, though, I am kind of a religious Muslim. Perhaps my personal belief of a higher power is not as defined as others would like, but I still consider myself Muslim. I still identify with the community. I still think it's important to me.

At the end of the day, in my opinion, religion is trying to understand the world around us, trying to understand the meaning of life. I'm very philosophical. In that sense, I'm thinking, "Okay, if I approach Islam as way of approaching life, a philosophy about life, meaning of life and how life works, are there some important values? And because I already have a cultural connection to Islam, are there some aspects of Islam that also connect me beyond just the culture?" That's when I think of concepts like charity, love, mercy, those aspects, and see the concept of God in them. To me, it's more inanimate, more like a force than like a being. It's interesting. I don't see it as supernatural. In that sense, some Muslims would ask, "Am I even Muslim anymore?" To me, I am Muslim. No one can tell me I'm not.

I can say, "God to me is a scientific or a physical inanimate force or like a universal force." I don't believe that saying this would go against anything within Islam, in my opinion, at least. Different people have different forms of their truth. This is how I see my truth; that is how I find ways to fit Islam into how I see the world in a way that works with me. I think what is valuable about religions is the fact religions tend to have many interpretations. I think one of the lasting values of religion is their being open. You have Sufis, you have Shias, you have Sunnis, you have Alawites, you have everything in between—all these different schools of thought. What I'm doing is just the individualized level of people exploring their faith and exploring what fits into their background, their faith. To me, this has been an individualized exploration of how I want to pursue my Muslim identity.

I had recently seen some debates online between two different Muslims. One of them was less practicing. As I was internet surfing, I saw different conversations within the Muslim community that were trying to create bridges across different Muslim communities. It might be Shias and Sunnis talking, between less religious and more religious Muslims, between ex-Muslims and Muslims even. It's important that people recognize that they have more in common than otherwise. We all come from the same community at the end of the day. Just because we all have a different opinion about our relationship with Islam, that doesn't mean any one group is anti-Muslim. I think you'll find more in common than otherwise inside the Muslim community. I just think it's important to focus on what we have in common rather than what we don't have in common. I think that's the thing I learned.

Ultimately, while at UVA, I have learned dialogue is extremely important. I have learned we should embrace differing opinions, not cancel people. I'm big about not canceling people. I think it is better instead to embed your voice into the space and welcome others into the dialogue. People are very receptive to dialogue. They don't fall into a psychological human state of self-defense, they don't dig into their opinions as opposed to if you were simply to attack them. When you attack, most of the time they are likely to not listen. It's important that people are welcomed in and then allowed to listen. If people are actively just coming against you, your first instinct is to defend yourself, defend your beliefs, and defend your rights. But if you're in a space where you have the privilege to talk and share opinions, then you should be open to talking, to challenging those views in a way that changes minds. I think the more people speak up, give different opinions, and bring different voices into UVA, our common spaces will change.

If I wanted to be as blunt as possible, I would say that UVA's a high-ranking school that focuses a lot on traditions, or at least still does so in many spaces of the university community. This is not necessarily a bad thing in the outset, and in many cases is a great thing, but the trade-off is whenever you have a place that considers tradition to be important, there comes the risk of being less welcoming of things that are different or things that are more liberal. I'm not saying UVA is illiberal, but I think UVA was once less welcoming of change, of different communities. Traditionally, I think, that has been the case with Muslims. I have heard comments that aren't blatantly racist per say but might be microaggressions based on not understanding Muslims or Islam. I think those tend to come more, in my opinion, from less diverse spaces where people might be more homogenous. Certain Greek life organizations are one example that might be dominated by one certain type of background, whether it's ethnic or socioeconomic, versus spaces like my experience at Hereford that tend to be more diverse in terms of backgrounds of students. So of course, given UVA has historically been dominated by a certain type of student, it is not surprising that traditionally UVA may have once had less understanding and had negative opinion of Islam or Muslims.

For me, diversity is having people from different backgrounds, different ethnic, racial, gender backgrounds. It's having different belief systems, could be religion, could be some politics. It's people from different socioeconomic statuses, people from all sorts of backgrounds, low-income or higher income, having both is useful. I think diversity brings a lot of richness to the community. You have so many different stories, so many different narratives that can explain a community's opinion and a community's understanding of a people, a certain faith group, and a certain people. To me, the more diverse, the better. On average, I've felt like more diversity was more accepting to me, not just at UVA, but in my adult life. In my opinion, the more diverse the space was, the more a nuanced idea of Islam existed in that space, a more accepting or a less one-sided "single story" idea of Islam existed. I think if you're in a space where people are different from you, then you can better understand or accept people who are different than you than if you just heard other stories. You've seen people from different places. It's almost like becoming just more educated or more understanding of people who are different. So, to me, this is the case of Muslims, I think.

As UVA continues to create a diverse student body, I can see, however small, changes that have been happening with understanding Muslims and Islam, and with an acceptance of the diversity within the UVA Muslim community itself. I think Muslim students might have been less accepted or less understood in the past, but I think the trend is going in the direction of UVA becoming more understanding and more accepting of Muslims.

"MY ADVICE TO FIRST YEARS AT A RECENT MSA EVENT: UVA'S MSA IS WHAT YOU MAKE IT"

Sumaya Mohammed
Class of 2023
School of Arts and Sciences

Sumaya Mohammed's narrative invites the reader into the experience of how one's experience can be shaped by the UVA Muslim Student Association (MSA). In particular, Sumaya discusses her experience of being a shy first year student to becoming Vice President of MSA. She discusses how she feels the organization has evolved and the many strides it has made since she joined. Mohammed also discusses how UVA should support different multicultural organizations to make a "better UVA."

Honestly, when I first even decided to come to UVA, I didn't like it at all. When I first visited, I didn't see any visibly Muslim people around me, or, just visibly POC people around me. It was a little difficult to even consider UVA. But UVA was also my best option, so I decided to come here. And then when I first arrived, my overall experience was pretty positive because, very early on, I found my own group of Muslim friends. My roommate was a friend from high school who was Muslim. Her best friend from middle school was also Muslim and at UVA. So, it was the three of us. The middle school's friend's roommate was also Muslim. So, then, there were four of us who were friends. I was able to create on my own Muslim environment.

We were all also visibly Muslim. We wore hijab. So, we were approached by more Muslims, especially those that wore the hijab. They tried to connect with us because when you're at a Predominantly White Institution, like UVA, you really try to look for and find the people that look like yourself. That's the most comforting thing you can have as a Muslim. That's something that's closest to home. I know my experience isn't true for everyone. And I wouldn't say that UVA's view and culture with regards to Islam, in terms of diversity and inclusion, is the best. Actually, it's not great. But because I found my group of friends so early and established myself in the Muslim community so early, I've had a positive experience. But that's not what everyone experiences.

If I did not come to UVA knowing someone, having friends, I think my experience would have been completely different. I tell this to my friends all the time. I say, "If we didn't decide to go to the MSA together for our first meeting, I don't think I would have ever been able to join." At that point in my life, I was extremely shy. I wasn't really the type of person to go to a new space where I don't know anyone and try to introduce myself. That just wasn't who I was at the time. Today, it's a different story, but back then, I was never like that. I definitely wouldn't have been able to find a Muslim space. Even if I did, I would have found that space much later in my life and not as early as I did.

During my first year, I was pretty close with my hallmates, who were mostly white. Without MSA, I would have been in that space a lot more. I probably would have lived with them the next year. My experience would have been the complete opposite. A lot of the social activities that my non-Muslim friends do, I don't necessarily take part in. So, if I only had them to hang out with, either I would have compromised my values to take part in those activities or I probably would have felt like I wasn't a part because I didn't take part in those activities. So as much as I enjoy my non-Muslim friends' company, I think it's more comforting to be around people that share similar values as mine, and I think UVA MSA has given me those people and the resources.

I feel like having those Muslim friends early on helped ground me in Islam as well. When you're in college, when you're away from home, I think it is really easy to forget your actual purpose and your deen. I think surrounding myself with Muslim friends earlier on really helped me ground myself in a place like UVA. Without a tight-knit community that keeps you grounded, it's really difficult to stay grounded and remember Islam. I think the real value of MSA is that students have been able to create a community for themselves and less that UVA has actively been working to make its university space inclusive for them.

I'm heavily involved in MSA. This year, I'm Vice-President, which allows me to do a lot of work. It helps me to reach out to first year students, because I know what it's like to come to UVA for the first time as a Muslim person. My motivation for being on the MSA Council was to try to find people like me during my first year at UVA. I've literally transformed since my first year in terms of my confidence, being able to speak in front of people, being able to socialize, and being able to make friends. I owe my self-image, how I think of myself, to my experiences in MSA. Being involved in MSA pushed me to get out of my comfort zone and connect with people. And those people have helped me become a better version of myself. They helped me both with my personal life and with my career.

I want first year students to come to an institution like UVA and have such resources. I want them to have someone who will say, "Hey, if you need anything, I'm here to help you." Or, "Hey, come join us. Let's grab lunch." I want to reach out to a lot of underclassmen so they can feel comfortable at UVA. That's what I've been trying to do. I have been trying to connect the first years, show them what UVA has to offer, help them see the good in most things that are here at UVA. That was my biggest motivation. MSA transformed me. I want people to experience the positive aspects of being in the UVA Muslim community.

For new Muslim students at UVA, when you get here, reach out to the UVA's Muslim Community. It's not perfect. It's really not. As with any community, we also have our issues. There's good and bad, but I think the good outweighs the bad. I would say reach out, try to connect with the community, and see what they have to offer. Come in with an open mind, without any assumptions or expectations. Most people hear a lot of things about Muslim communities at universities. There's a lot of stereotypes that go around. There's a lot of rumors, a lot of gossiping, about MSA. "People join MSA because they're trying to find a spouse." "MSA is toxic." "People are judgmental." "Everyone's cliquey." I mean I have experienced all of these moments. I have experienced people that are judgmental, but I've also experienced amazing people that have helped me out in a lot of unexpected ways.

Like I said earlier, you find what you look for. If you come with an open mind, you can find the right people. If you come with expectations, then you attract what you look for, to be honest. If you're like, "Oh, I'm going to meet good people that are going to help me," then you're most likely going to find those people. My advice to first years at a recent MSA event was "UVA's MSA is what you make it." If you choose to come with an open mind hoping to meet people, you're literally going to make your best friends here. It's going to help you stay grounded both academically and in your deen. But if you come with stereotypes, expectations, and misconceptions of what it's going to be or what it's going to look like, that's what you're going to get because there's both in the community. You get what you look for at UVA and MSA.

When I first heard about the letter to MSA expressing concerns about its representing the complexity of the UVA Muslim community or its lack thereof, as a Black Muslim myself, I agreed with a lot of the student concerns. I was at the post-letter meeting held by MSA. I was there listening to everyone. In terms of inclusivity, when it comes to Black Muslims, Shia Muslims, or minority groups within the community, MSA was lacking. It's predominantly Desi, predominantly Arab. So, we do have a lot to improve. We talk about this at the beginning of every year. We set goals and expectations. A lot of the issues in the statement resonated with me. That was one of my motivations for joining the MSA Council. I've had a lot of positive experiences, but then that doesn't negate a lot of negative experiences other people might have had.

One of my goals was to try and change those negative experiences. MSA is a lot different now. I won't say it's perfect, because we still have issues that we need to fix. It's a lot better, though, than it was in our first year because we see a lot of Shia Muslims involved in MSA, and a lot more Black people involved in the MSA. I now see a lot of non-hijabis feeling comfortable coming to the MSA because they don't feel scrutinized. It's getting a lot better. I won't say it's perfect, but it's definitely getting better. I hope it goes up from there. Working with Muslims United and Black Muslims at UVA is a unique experience to be honest. A lot of the new Muslim spaces and the leaders of those Muslim spaces are my friends. At the moment we're trying to move on from the past and create a more positive working relationship.

As a result of all this work, I think MSA is a little bit more evolved. We needed to understand that the Muslim identity isn't limited at all to a set of identity groups. The Muslim community is really diverse. We understand that some practices are unique to certain sects so we try not to generalize, and stay mindful of the spaces we occupy. When we host Taraweeh prayers during Ramadan, we understood that Shia Muslims would not take part, so we made a separate group chat where we announce these events without spamming the main group chat which reaches everyone in MSA. When we have Shia holidays that Sunnis don't necessarily celebrate, we do informational sessions. We teach everyone about these Shia practices because most people don't know a lot of the history that we share.

Most people don't even understand where the conflict comes from because we're all Muslims in the end, right? We share our biggest identity as Muslims even if certain ways in which we practice may be different. Understanding our differences makes us more appreciative of each other. This is why we host educational events. This year we did an event for Ar'baeen. One of our council members is a Shia Muslim and she hosted an educational session. We had a pretty high turnout. We had people that identify as Sunni and those that identify as Shia come to learn about Ar'baeen, what it means to the Shia community and what we all, as Muslims, can learn from it.

This year we are definitely trying to expand our outreach, and we're trying to work with multicultural organizations. We're trying to plan events with organizations like EESA, BSA, OAS and many more. We're really trying to branch out so we can connect with Muslims that may not necessarily be a part of the MSA, who might not feel included. We're trying to reach out to individuals who take part in other organizations because they feel like their identity is most reflected in those organizations. We want to show them that MSA is a space for them, too. It's definitely not going to be a one-year project. Not everything is going to change in a year or two.

My hope as a Council Representative is to at least start the process and, then, continue working so it gets better and better until people feel more included. And I've definitely seen a difference. I won't say we are free from all issues, but I will say that it's definitely gotten better. I won't necessarily say we have addressed all the issues in the letter because a lot of the grievances aren't something that can be fixed overnight. It's an institutional issue, so it's going to take time to actually address those grievances, in terms of inclusivity, for instance. It's going to take time for people to trust that MSA is a space for them, too. They have to see continuous effort from our end, and that's what we're trying to show them.

Honestly, I would also like to see UVA actively supporting organizations like MSA, BSA, and multicultural student organizations more broadly. I would like to see them pour money into these organizations, advertise them, and reach out specifically to POC. I would like them to reach out not just to reach a quota, but to actively get talented students that can make UVA better. Then, in terms of recruitment, I'd love to see UVA recruit more people that look like me. Not just in terms of Islam, but as a Black person, as an immigrant, as a woman. I feel when I walk on Grounds, all I see are white men and white women. I don't see people that look like me. Hijabis, non-hijabis, Black women, I want to be surrounded with people that look like me, too, so that I feel like I belong. This year has been a little different. I was telling my friends the other day, "Guys, I was walking around, and I saw so many POC, and that made me so happy. I have never seen that. I was walking to class and I saw so many POC on-Grounds." That was just so abnormal. I was like, "Whoa, this is so weird." It's not supposed to be weird. It should be normal.

The Muslim community is what defines my experience at UVA, from classes I've taken for my major to deciding on focusing on Public Health. A lot of people told me to apply. I didn't think I was going to do public health. I was just taking biology. Then a lot of my peers told me to apply, so I was like,

"Let me just apply to Public Health." Then I got accepted. So now I'm doing a double major in Biology and Public Health. It shows that a lot of aspects of my college life have been influenced by the people around me. And the people around me have been predominantly Muslim. In terms of my personal growth and my relationship to Islam, I feel like MSA has really helped me stay grounded. MSA has given me those people and the resources.

With MSA, honestly, this is cliché, but it's always the people. Let's say I'm really stressed with an exam and I'm in a library. Then I see a friend that comes in. Then we're both sitting, stressing out together. Then another friend comes, then another friend comes. Then all of a sudden, it's like six, seven people squeezed into a booth. You are not alone. You are in a community. You know how when you're with your family, you're just talking about random stuff and just laughing, just goofing around? I grew up with a really big family. Then when I moved to the U.S., I didn't have that anymore. I was not in a good place because of that distance. But when I got to UVA, I basically found my second family. The things I experienced growing up with my cousins, with my siblings, I was now able to experience here. It really feels like home to me because my house was chaotic and my UVA experience has also been chaotic. The people around me are chaotic. In that sense, it does remind me of home.

Afterword

Oludamini Ogunnaike
Associate Professor of African Religious Thought and
Democracy
Dept. of Religious Studies, University of Virginia

It is a curious thing to work for an institution at whose founding you would have been enslaved, to teach in halls and buildings named after renowned scientists who dedicated much of their lives to proving your "intellectual and moral inferiority." Teaching and working at an institution that strongly resisted the admission of faculty and students of your background well into the 1970's and even 1980's is a curious thing indeed. When walking on the Grounds of the University of Virginia, I often think of the hands that first dug the foundations, laid the brick walls, and served the early students and faculty of this institution. Most likely some of those hands embraced the earth in prostration and were held to the heavens in supplication in the same rituals in which I and many of the students' whose voices are recorded in this volume partake multiple times a day. These hands helped build this institution, but this institution was not built for them,[1] nor for their descendants.

A few generations later, the university is still struggling to overcome this legacy. The fact that the university's structures and cultures were designed to serve a very specific kind of person (white, Christian or post-Christian, moneyed men, and later, women) has meant that these structures and cultures have been hostile in ways both obvious and subtle, intentional and unintentional, to those who diverge from that assumed norm. "Diversifying" UVA, or rather removing its unjust and prejudicial barriers to entrance, is only a small part of the process of redress, which must also transform these institutional structures and cultures. Not doing so is tantamount to planting tropical trees in the desert. As many of the students in this volume eloquently articulate, the environment must also be transformed. Such transformations must not be mistaken for a kind of "pandering" to student identity groups, but rather a precious opportunity for academic institutions and their cultures to face themselves and their world honestly, to critically confront and shed their long-held bigotries and open themselves to a deeper understanding of themselves, their history, and the world at large. But this understanding cannot be achieved without such reckoning and transformation.

As I read through these carefully collected records of Muslim students' experiences of and reflections on their time at UVA, I was struck by two things: firstly, the ways in which some Muslim student experiences and demands mirror those of Black students from the 1970's[2] to the 2010's[3] and 20's.[4] Secondly, I was struck by the difference in tone of these students' responses to my own when faced with similar aggravations from faculty, students, and staff. It took me a while to put my finger on what this difference was, and then it suddenly struck me: these students expected to feel just as welcomed in this university as their non-Muslim, white peers. Immigrating to the United States from Nigeria as a child, I was raised with the expectation that I was and would always be somewhat of a "stranger," that the institutions of this country were not made for me, and that while I should not always accept prejudicial and discriminatory treatment, I should expect it. While such low expectations saved me much heartache and disappointment, it is a beautiful thing to witness that this next generation of students has higher expectations of their universities and peers.

As a professor in the Religious Studies Dept. at UVA, I have not had the same experiences as these students, nor do I agree with all of their complaints and recommendations. However, since I was hired by UVA in 2019, I have served as a faculty advisor to the Muslim Students' Association, and for the few months before COVID forced us online, witnessed firsthand many of the dynamics and incidents to which the students refer in this volume. In my office hours and informal conversations with Muslim students, many expressed their frustration with having to "defend Islam and Muslims" from some of the uninformed prejudices, uncritical assumptions, and factual errors of their professors and classmates, not to mention the outright hostility and harassment some of them faced. Because of the current political climate, it has become common for media pundits, politicians, and even professors to make statements about Muslims that would be nearly unthinkable about any other group. Although some might like to imagine otherwise, academia is far from free of such prejudices. To add but one personal example to those shared by the students in this volume, many years ago, a member of a search committee for a position at another university to which I was applying told me that one faculty member was worried that I was "too Muslim" to teach Islamic studies at their institution. Could you imagine someone being criticized for being "too African" to teach African studies, "too Jewish" to teach Judaic studies, or "too much of a Kantian" to teach philosophy? This is the kind of difficult climate that Muslim students at UVA have been facing. The short-lived Muslim chaplaincy program at the university filled an important need for Muslim students that neither faculty nor peers could really offer—a culturally and religiously-competent, confidential counselor who helped students individually and collectively navigate and integrate their spiritual, academic, and social realities in various ways.

While it may be tempting for some to dismiss this volume as the complaints of "overly-sensitive" or "ungrateful" students, I would like to call attention to the words of the editors of this volume in its introduction, which bear repeating here at its end, "Students don't speak out against UVA because they hate UVA. They speak out because they love UVA. They are willing to criticize, speak out, and face backlash, so they can create a better university not only for future Muslim students and minority students, but for all students."[5] If the University truly wants to become "great and good," it is important to take such student experiences and voices into careful consideration. This does not mean uncritically acquiescing to any and all student demands, but rather making a serious effort to listen to and understand the conditions that give rise to these complaints. The University of Virginia has a long and often violent history of white supremacy, from its founding in 1819 to the neo-Nazi riots of 2017. I do not know what kinds of programs and initiatives are necessary to transform UVA into a fair and just institution where students, faculty, and staff of all backgrounds can thrive. I do not know how to build a future that rights the wrongs perpetrated by our institution in both the past and present. However, I do know a little bit about how this university reached its present state from its past, and that has only been made possible by the incredibly difficult work of organizing and advocacy among students, faculty, staff, and community members to make their voices heard and to make the University better for all. For this reason, it is important to hear, to understand, and to consider thoughtfully the student perspectives collected in this volume.

Notes

1. In fact, one of the reasons Thomas Jefferson gave for the founding of the University of Virginia was the defense of slavery and the southern economy and way of life based upon it from Northern abolitionist movements: "In its inception, even in Jefferson's own imagining of what the University of Virginia could be, he understood it to be an institution with slavery at its core, both in how it functioned and what its purpose was. He believed that a southern institution was necessary to protect the sons of the South from the abolitionist teachings of the North. Jefferson wrote to his friend James Breckinridge and expressed his concern with sending the youth of Virginia to be educated in the North, a place 'against us in position and principle.' He worried that in northern institutions young Virginians might imbibe 'opinions and principles in discord with those of his own country. [T]his canker is eating on the vitals of our existence, and if not arrested at once will be beyond remedy.' In other words, Jefferson believed it was important to educate Virginians and other southerners in an institution that understood and ultimately supported slavery." ("President's Commission on Slavery and the University: Report to President Teresa A. Sullivan, 2018", 15).

2. In 1972, The Black Student Alliance drafted a letter entitled "Directives and Proposals to the President and the Board of Visitors." See "An Epoch of Change: a timeline of the university 1955-1975" http://xroads.virginia.edu/~ug03/omara-alwala/Harrison/Timeline.html, Last Accessed 09/14/2022.

3. David Mack, "Black Students At UVA: 'We Have To Do Something,'" BuzzfeedNews, March 23rd 2015, https://www.buzzfeednews.com/article/davidmack/black-students-at-uva-we-have-to-do-something, Last accessed 09/14/2022; Jeremy Bauer Wolf, " UVA Minority Groups Demand Changes" Inside Higher Ed, Sep. 1st, 2017. https://www.insidehighered.com/quicktakes/2017/09/01/uva-minority-groups-demand-changes. Last accessed 09/14/2022; Maria Danilova, "After Charlottesville, students worry about safety on campus" PBS NewsHour, August 19th, 2017. https://www.pbs.org/newshour/nation/charlottesville-students-worry-safety-campus, Last Accessed 09/14/2022 ; Wes Gobar, "What it's like to be a Black student as white supremacists march in your college town," Vox, March 19th, 2017, https://www.vox.com/first-person/2017/5/19/15663516/robert-e-lee-statue-charlottesville-richard-spencer, Last Accessed 09/14/2022.

4. Nick Anderson and Susan Svrluga "From Slavery to Jim Crow to George Floyd: Vir-

ginia universities face a long racial reckoning" The Washington Post Nov. 26th, 2021. https://www.washingtonpost.com/education/2021/11/26/virginia-universities-slavery-race-reckoning/, Last Accessed 09/14/2022

5. In this, the editors of the present volume echo the sentiments of some of the first Black students at UVA, who in a 1969 recruitment pamphlet for potential applicants, wrote, "The University of Virginia will be more meaningful to Black people—in fact, all people—if the Black students make it so." (quoted in Ernie Gates, "Integrating from Behind the Scenes" Virginia Magazine (Summer 2017), https://uvamagazine.org/articles/integrating_from_behind_the_scenes, Last Accessed 09/14/2022.

Glossary of Key Terms

Abd'Llah Al-Ansari, Imam
Islamic Society of Central Virginia (ISVC), Charlottesville, VA

Alawite
The word Alawite is the anglicized version of *'alawī*, an attribute of allegiance to ʿAlī the cousin and son-in-law of the Prophet Muhammad. Alawites follows a Shia interpretation of Islam but depart from other Shias in distinct ways. For example, the general view of Shia Muslims is that succession in Islam should be based upon bloodlines therefore, making ʿAlī the Prophet's natural successor. The Alawites take the veneration of ʿAlī a step further and allegedly invest him with divine attributes.

al-ḥamdulillāh
An Arabo-Islamic expression comprised of three words: *al-ḥamd*, *lī*, and Allah which literally means "all praise belongs to God".

Arba'een
A Shia religious observance that is celebrated 40 days after the day of Ashura to commemorate the death of Hussein bin Ali, Grandson of Prophet Muhammad.

as-salāmu 'alaikum
Another Arabo-Islamic expression which means "peace be upon you".

ʿīd

The word ʿīd (often anglicized "eid") is an Arabic word that conveys the meaning of festival, holiday, or celebration. There are two ʿīds celebrated by all Muslims, ʿīdul-fiṭr (the festival of fast breaking) and ʿīdul-adḥā (the festival of sacrifice).

ḥadīth

In Islamic terminology the word ḥadīth refers to individual recorded accounts of the sayings of the Prophet Muhammad, his daily practices, his tacit approvals, his physical characteristics, and or his moral character. It is also often used to refer to the corpus of these accounts.

ḥalaqah

Literally "a circle". This word is often used in Arabo-Islamic culture to refer to a circle of learning most often – but not necessarily – held in a mosque (Muslim house of worship).

ḥijāb

An Islamic term that comes from the Arabic verb ḥajaba which means to cover or conceal. The word ḥijāb is often used erroneously as a synonym for kimār (head scarf), but is actually more comprehensive, referring to the standard of modesty observed by practicing Muslim women and the entirety of garments worn by them to achieve this standard.

ḥijābī

In the common vernacular of lay Muslims refers to a Muslim woman who actively wears a head scarf in public to cover her hair, ears, neck, and bosom, or some combination of these.

iftār

Another Arabo-Islamic term that means "fast breaking" and also doubles as a name for the meal consumed by Muslims upon completing a day of fasting.

īmān

An Islamic term that means faith or belief and comprises conviction in the heart, corresponding expressions with the tongue (e.g., there is no deity worthy of worship except Allah and Muhammad is His Messenger), and affirming deeds carried out by the limbs (e.g., ritual prayer, almsgiving, fasting, etc.).

Imām Hussain

Hussain bin ʿAlī is the grandson of the Prophet Muhammad. In Shia Islam he is venerated as the third of their 12 imams. Imam Hussain is revered by both Sunni and Shia Muslims, but he is centrally important to most Shia theologies.

in shāʾ Allāh

Another Arabo-Islamic term which means "if it be God's will" or "God willing".

Islamic Society of Central Virginia (ISVC)

The first masjid (mosque) in historic Charlottesville, Virginia. The UVA Muslim Community regularly works with the ISVC on many events throughout the year.

Jumuʿah

Literally, "Friday". In Islamic terminology it refers to the congregational worship service, mandatory upon resident Muslim males, and held at midday every Friday in a mosque or similar space.

PBUH/Peace Be Upon Him

The English translation of the words *ṣallallāhu ʿalaihi wa sallam*, commonly said by Muslims, out of respect, after mentioning the name of the Prophet or his title.

Quran

This Islamic term literally means "the oft-recited" and refers to the divine revelation received by the Prophet Muhammad piecemeal, as dictated by the circumstances, over a span of 23 years. For Muslims the Qur'ān is the literal word of God, the primary source for Islamic law, and God's final testament to humanity. Reciting it is both an act of worship and an integral part of ritual prayer.

Ramadan
The 9th month of lunar-Islamic calendar and the month designated for ritual fasting in Islam. throughout the month of Ramadan Muslims all over the world observe a dry fast, abstaining from eating, drinking, and intercourse from dawn until dusk.

Shia
A term used to refer to the followers of the second major theological sect of Muslims. There are several subsects which ascribe to Shiism. Shia Muslims contend with "Sunni" Muslims on a variety of issues and some of their subsects – despite these contentions – are close to mainstream Sunni Islam while others are very far away on issues ranging from theology to political structure, to ritual practice, and so on.

Sufism
The Arabic words *ṣūfī* and *at-taṣawwuf* are derived from the word *ṣūf* which means wool and *ṣūfī* which means woolen. The term was originally used for highly devout individuals and ascetics. Over time it came to refer to a more mystical approach to practicing Islam that emphasized unfettered spirituality, sainthood, the veneration of saints, and esotericism.

suḥūr
The term used to refer to the pre-dawn meal consumed by Muslims as a part of ritual fasting. Muslims are encouraged to eat something before initiating the fast each day in Ramadan and when performing voluntary fasts outside of Ramadan.

Sunnah

This is an Islamic term which conveys one of four meanings depending on the context in which it is used. In the context of theology, it refers to orthodoxy as opposed to heretical and unprecedented theological perspectives. In the context of jurisprudence, it refers to religious practices which are recommended or highly virtuous and commendable. In the context of *ḥadīth* terminology, it refers to any and all statements, actions, and tacit approvals attributed to the Prophet as well as descriptions of him or his character (i.e., a near synonym for *ḥadīth*). In the context of Islamic disciplines and sciences, it refers to the source of Islamic law second only to the Qur'ān in authority.

Sunnī

An attributive title derived from the word "Sunnah" and indicates a commitment to following the tradition or "way" of the Prophet Muhammad and or his immediate successors. This term is commonly used to distinguish between the two major theological Muslim sects, the followers of "Sunnah" or Sunnis and the Shia.

Editor Biographies

Wafa Salah, Class of 2021

Wafa Salah graduated from the University of Virginia in 2021 with a B.A. in Cognitive Science and a concentration in Computer Science. She is on the pre-health track and working to join medical school. As a hijabi Muslim in the United States and a student at a P.W.I., she helped conceive this project with the hopes of creating a platform that would amplify the voices of the students in her community. Exhausted by the media's consistent distorted portrayal of her Islamic identity, Wafa feels a strong sense of urgency for Muslims to take back control of their narrative. By owning their stories and sharing their perspectives, she believes that Muslims can change the misrepresentations by which the western world not only perceives them but also depicts them to the rest of the world.

During her time at UVA, Wafa conducted biomedical research as part of the Dutta Lab in UVA's School of Medicine. She was a USOAR and Echols scholar, and served on the MSA Council as Sister's Coordinator in the 2020-2021 academic year. Among her other commitments, she found great fulfillment through her volunteer work in Madison House and as a teaching assistant for Organic Chemistry. In her spare time, she enjoys playing volleyball and having meaningful conversations on topics including astronomy, philosophy, culture, religion, and various social issues. She is also a huge football (soccer) fan!

Fawzia Tahsin, Class of 2023

Fawzia Tahsin is an undergraduate student at the McIntire School of Commerce, University of Virginia. She is a double major pursuing a B.S. in Commerce with a concentration in IT and a track in Business Analytics as well as Global Studies with a concentration in Global Public Health. As a former research student under the UVA Office of Undergraduate Research, she was motivated to join this project to share oral histories about being Muslim at UVA, as her own experience of being a female Muslim student of color has resonated with the stories presented throughout the book. She wishes to challenge the status quo, stand up for minority rights, and create meaningful strategies for social progress within UVA grounds and beyond.

Fawzia also holds many leadership positions such as Co-Executive Director for the Muslim Institute for Leadership and Empowerment (MILE) in the 2022-23 school year, and a peer mentor for the McIntire Commerce Cohort Program. She also holds many honors being a McIntire Commerce Cohort recipient, UVA Rainey Scholar, Harrison Grant Recipient, UVA's Race, Religion, and Democracy Lab Cohort member, USOAR scholar, and QuestBridge Scholar.

Beyond academics, Fawzia loves to cook delicious homemade meals, go on food outings with her friends, sing along to classic Disney soundtracks, and watch the latest romantic comedies on Netflix.